READ FOR REAL

Nonfiction Strategies for Reading Results

Authors

Leslie W. Crawford, Ed.D.
Professor of Literacy
Georgia College & State University

Charles E. Martin, Ph.D.
Professor of Early Childhood and Middle Grades Education
Georgia College & State University

Vocabulary and Fluency Consultant

Timothy V. Rasinski, Ph.D.
Professor of Education
Kent State University

English Language Learner Specialist

Caroline Teresa Linse, Ed.D.
Fulbright Scholar
Minsk State Linguistic University
Minsk, Belarus

Zaner-Bloser

Photo Credits

ISBN 978-07367-7339-3

Copyright © 2011 Zaner-Bloser, Inc.

Zaner-Bloser, Inc., P.O. Box 16764, Columbus, Ohio 43216-6764 (1-800-421-3018)

Printed in the United States of America

11 12 13 14 25170 5 4 3 2

Certified Chain of Custody
Promoting Sustainable
Forest Management
www.sfiprogram.org

Table of Contents

Table of Contents (continued)

Unit 5: The Changing Earth

Unit 6: Pioneers in Technology

Hi! We're your

Reading Team Partners!

Have you noticed that the reading you do in science and social studies is different from reading stories and novels? Reading nonfiction <u>is</u> different. When you read nonfiction, you learn new information. We'll introduce you to some strategies that will help you read and understand nonfiction.

In each unit, you'll learn three strategies—one to use **Before** you read, one to use **During** your reading, and one to use **After** you read. You'll work with these strategies in all three reading selections in each unit.

In the first selection, you'll **Learn** the unit strategies. When you see a red button like this ◉, read "My Thinking" notes to see how one of us modeled the strategy.

In the second selection in each unit, you'll **Practice** the strategies by jotting down your own notes about how you used the same unit strategies. The red button ◉ will tell you where to stop and think about the strategies.

When you read the last selection in each unit, you'll **Apply** the strategies. You'll decide when to stop and take notes as you read.

Strategies

Here they are—the **Before, During,** and **After** Reading Strategies.

Use these strategies with all your nonfiction reading—social studies and science textbooks, magazine and newspaper articles, Web sites, and more.

Now that you've met the team, it's time to get started.

	BEFORE READING	DURING READING	AFTER READING
UNIT 1	**Preview the Selection** by looking at the title and headings to predict what the selection will be about.	**Make Connections** by relating information that I already know about the subject to what I'm reading.	**Recall** by summarizing the selection in writing or out loud.
UNIT 2	**Activate Prior Knowledge** by looking at the title, headings, pictures, and graphics to decide what I know about this topic.	**Interact With Text** by identifying the main idea and supporting details.	**Evaluate** by searching the selection to determine how the author used evidence to reach conclusions.
UNIT 3	**Set a Purpose** by using the title and headings to write questions that I can answer while I am reading.	**Clarify Understanding** by using photographs, charts, and other graphics to help me understand what I'm reading.	**Respond** by drawing logical conclusions about the topic.
UNIT 4	**Preview the Selection** by looking at the photographs, illustrations, captions, and graphics to predict what the selection will be about.	**Make Connections** by comparing my experiences with what I'm reading.	**Recall** by using the headings to question myself about what I read.
UNIT 5	**Activate Prior Knowledge** by reading the introduction and/or summary to decide what I know about this topic.	**Interact With Text** by identifying how the text is organized.	**Evaluate** by forming a judgment about whether the selection was objective or biased.
UNIT 6	**Set a Purpose** by skimming the selection to decide what I want to know about this subject.	**Clarify Understanding** by deciding whether the information I'm reading is fact or opinion.	**Respond** by forming my own opinion about what I've read.

Unit 1
Strategies

BEFORE READING

Preview the Selection

by looking at the title and headings to predict what the selection will be about.

DURING READING

Make Connections

by relating information that I already know about the subject to what I'm reading.

AFTER READING

Recall

by summarizing the selection in writing or out loud.

LEARN
the strategies
in the selection
**Cockroaches:
The Ultimate Survivors**
page 11

PRACTICE
the *strategies*
in the selection
Deep-Sea Monster
page 25

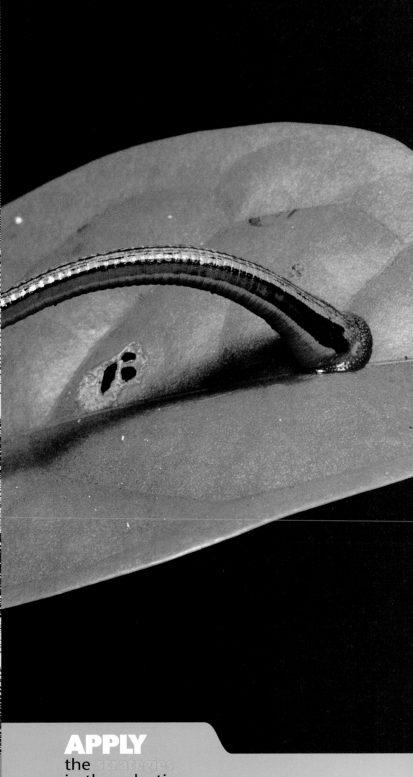

APPLY
the *strategies*
in the selection
The Remarkable Leech
page 37

Think About the Strategies

BEFORE READING

Preview the Selection

by looking at the title and headings to predict what the selection will be about.

My Thinking

This strategy says to preview the selection by looking at the title and headings to predict what the selection will be about. The title tells me I am going to be reading about cockroaches, and it says they are the "ultimate survivors." I wonder what that means.

From the headings, I predict that I am going to learn about where cockroaches live, what they look like, how they multiply, what they eat, and why they are important to humans. There is a lot to learn about the cockroach!

DURING READING

Make Connections

by relating information that I already know about the subject to what I'm reading.

My Thinking

The strategy says to make connections to the selection by relating information I already know about the subject to what I'm reading. I will stop and think about this strategy every time I come to a red button like this ⊙.

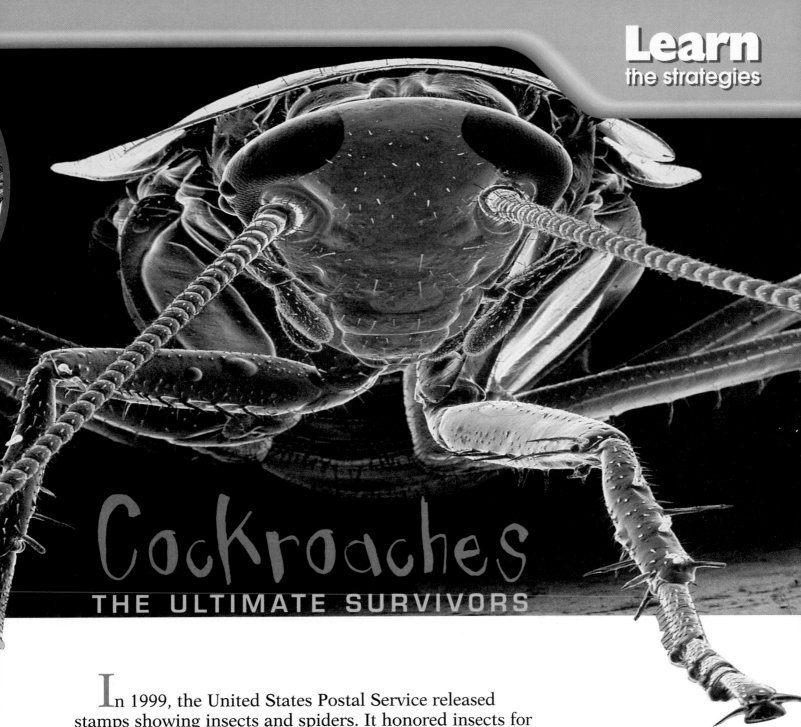

Cockroaches
THE ULTIMATE SURVIVORS

In 1999, the United States Postal Service released stamps showing insects and spiders. It honored insects for their survival skills and importance in nature. The lady beetle, flower fly, and katydid got stamps. The cockroach did not.

"Well, that makes sense," you may be thinking. "Cockroaches are a major **nuisance**. They don't deserve to be on a postage stamp, right?" Many people feel the same way. What they don't know is that the same cockroaches that are pests in our homes are very useful to scientists in their labs.

Vo•cab•u•lar•y

nuisance (noo•suhns)— something that is an annoyance; a bother

[11]

Cockroach Basics

Insects may be the most successful living creatures in the world. If this is so, roaches must be the most **enduring** insects. They have lived on the earth for more than 350 million years. In all that time, they have changed very little. Today, there are more than 3,500 different kinds of roaches in the world. As many as 57 kinds live in North America alone!

The roach is related to the termite and the praying mantis. The praying mantis may be its closest relative. However, there still are basic differences. For example, the roach will eat anything, but the praying mantis eats only meat.

The cockroach is so common that every language has a word for it. Our word comes from the Spanish word *cucaracha* [koo•kuh•**rah**•chuh]. Early English settlers changed the word a little. They made it sound like two words they knew: *cock* (another word for rooster) and *roach* (a fish that lives in ponds and lakes).

Oriental cockroach

Where Roaches Live

Roaches like warm weather, so most of them live in the warmer areas of North America. The three kinds that live closest to people are the American cockroach, the German cockroach, and the Oriental cockroach. They live in homes, factories, warehouses, restaurants, and even hospitals. These roaches rarely go outdoors. Both the Oriental roach and the German roach are **native** worldwide. The American roach is native from Florida to Mexico. However, it will live anywhere indoors, as long as it is indoors. It will even live in Antarctica if it gets carried there! As long as the indoor temperature is over 65°F and there is water, the cockroach can survive.

Vo•cab•u•lar•y

enduring—lasting; surviving

native (**nay**•tiv)—born in a particular place or country

Many kinds of roaches live near water or in damp places, such as a basement or under a sink. Roaches live in groups, but they don't work together as ants do.

What Roaches Look Like

Like all insects, the cockroach has three pairs of legs and no backbone. Cockroaches are **arthropods**. Arthropods have jointed legs and segmented bodies. Most roaches have three joints in each leg. Cockroaches also have an **exoskeleton**. An exoskeleton is a hard skeleton that is outside the body and covers it. The roach's exoskeleton is called the chitin. As the roach grows, it sheds its chitin and makes a new one.

Giant Brazilian cockroaches

Roaches have a flat, oval body. Of the varieties found in the United States, the German roach is the smallest. It is rarely more than five-eighths inch long. The American roach is the largest roach found in the United States. It may grow to be two inches long! All roaches have long **antennae,** slender feelers on their heads. They use their antennae to smell. The leg bristles—short, stiff hairs—give them their sense of touch.

The Oriental roach is brown or black. The American roach is reddish brown with yellow-brown edges. The German roach is light or dark brown. Other kinds of

American cockroach

Vo•**cab**•u•lar•y

arthropods (**ar**•thruh•podz)— any of a group of animals that have jointed legs and bodies made of segments

exoskeleton (ek•soh•**skel**•i•tuhn)—a hard outer structure that provides protection for the body

antennae (an•**ten**•ee)— pairs of thin moving organs on the head of insects or animals

[13]

roaches are also black, brown, gray, bright green, yellow, red, or orange. The brightly colored ones live in the tropics and can be as much as five inches long!

Most roaches have wings that fold across their backs. The common roaches don't fly very often, but they are amazingly fast on their feet. Many people don't know that roaches live in their homes until they turn on a light at night and see one quickly disappear into a crack.

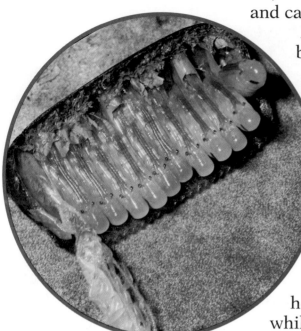

Opened roach
egg case with eggs

The Roach's Body

Roaches have white blood. They don't have lungs. To breathe, they take in air through **spiracles**. Spiracles are tiny holes in the sides of their bodies that send air to the other parts of the body. Roaches can live for more than half an hour without breathing. They can also live for a while if their hearts don't work. Even if they lose their heads, their bodies will continue to live until they become **dehydrated**.

Because most cockroaches are **repelled** by light, they live in dark places. Roaches spend the daytime hiding in cracks. They come out at nighttime to eat.

How Roaches Multiply and Grow

Female roaches lay eggs in egg cases. As many as 60 eggs may be in one case. Some roaches carry their egg case around for several days before leaving it somewhere. Female German roaches mate just once in their lives. When they do, they get enough sperm from the male to fertilize eggs for an entire lifetime. Some African cockroach females can actually **clone** themselves. They **reproduce** without mating at all!

Once hatched, roaches take care of themselves from the very start of their lives. A young cockroach sheds its skin between 5 and 14 times before becoming an adult. The German cockroach sheds its skin about 6 times in the 3 months that it takes to become an adult. The American cockroach becomes an adult in about 7 months. Adult cockroaches live for as little as a single month or for as long as several years.

Vo·cab·u·lar·y

spiracles (**spir**•uh•kuhlz)— tiny holes in the exoskeleton of insects

dehydrated (dee•**hy**•dray•tid)—dry; without water

repelled (ri•**peld**)—kept away

clone (klohn)—to make an exact copy of

reproduce (ree•pruh•**doos**)— to make offspring

[14]

Cockroaches eat anything—even pizza!

What Roaches Eat

Roaches have strong jaws that let them eat anything. They eat crumbs that are too small to see. They eat pet food and garbage. They will even eat makeup and the glue in book bindings! Much of the water they need comes from their food. While they can live for a whole month without eating, they need water at least once a week. Just one drop of water is enough.

It is not uncommon for insects to eat other kinds of insects. But some eat other roaches. Roaches even eat dead roaches. If there isn't any other food around, they'll even eat other living roaches!

Weird Roaches

Some roaches are very strange. A giant cockroach in Central America and the Caribbean lives in trees, in logs, and in caves with bats. The young roaches dig into the droppings of the bats.

The Madagascar hissing cockroach makes a loud buzzerlike noise. It has no wings and lives along the banks of rivers.

The Madeira roach uses odor as a defense. Most roaches give off a smell, especially when they mate. When threatened, the Madeira roach really stinks!

Most roaches lay eggs, but one kind of tropical roach bears its offspring live. These roaches spend several days with their mothers before going off into the world.

Why Roaches Are Important to Study

Why is learning about the cockroach important? **Entomologists** are scientists who study insects. When they study cockroaches and other insects, they learn things about them that might be useful. These scientists like to study the cockroach in particular because it is a survivor. Cockroaches will stay alive during harsh conditions. They don't need anything special to survive. Remember, unlike other insects, they eat just about anything. (Fleas, for example, eat only blood.) And, cockroaches multiply very quickly.

By studying the cockroach, entomologists have learned certain behaviors about cockroaches. They have learned that cockroaches don't find their way through a maze as easily as ants do. However, cockroaches do seem to have better memories than ants. Entomologists have also learned that cockroaches that live outside pick up and spread pollen. In what ways has learning about cockroaches' memories and how they spread **pollen** helped us?

Help for Humans

Because roaches can remember, some scientists hope they can be trained to take tiny cameras or other instruments into out-of-the-way places in buildings. This would be very helpful because it would let people see places they can't look at otherwise. For example, after a natural disaster, such as an earthquake, these cameras could help engineers find small dangerous cracks in buildings.

Vo • cab • u • lar • y

entomologists (en•tuh•**mol**•uh•jists)— scientists who study insects

pollen (**pol**•uhn)—yellow powder in flowering plants

Because cockroaches are extremely sensitive to **vibration,** they have been used in earthquake research. In one study, cockroaches were placed in boxes near three California sites that have experienced earthquakes. Just before the earthquakes, the cockroaches got very active. These results made scientists wonder if cockroaches might be useful in predicting earthquakes.

Attached to a high-tech "backpack," a cockroach helps scientists with earthquake predictions.

Balancing Nature

Although many cockroaches are found indoors, most kinds of roaches actually live outdoors. Some live under rotten logs and in tree stumps. In a rain forest, many live in the tops of trees. These outdoor roaches feed on dead plants and animals. They are important **recyclers**.

Some cockroaches also help plants **pollinate**. As they move across plants, feeding on dead and live leaves, they pick up and spread pollen. That helps the plants reproduce. Learning about how cockroaches pollinate helps us learn how certain plants and crops grow.

A green tree roach

Strategy

Make Connections by relating information that I already know about the subject to what I'm reading.

My Thinking
I am glad cockroaches are so helpful. I am also a good recycler. I always put bottles, cans, and papers in the recycling bins. But I didn't know that cockroaches could recycle, too!

Vo•**cab**•u•lar•y

vibration (vy•**bray**•shuhn)— quivering; rapid back-and-forth motion

recyclers (ree•**sy**•kluhrz)— those who reuse useful materials from waste

pollinate (**pol**•uh•nayt)— to transfer pollen

Vo·cab·u·lar·y

asthma (**az**•muh)—a disease that causes difficulty breathing and coughing

insecticides (in•**sek**•ti•sydz)—poisonous chemicals

Using Text Features

Chart According to the chart, how do cockroaches spend most of their time? About how many hours are cockroaches active each day?

Answer: Cockroaches spend 75% of the time resting. That means they are active 25% (about 6 hours) of each 24-hour day.

If Roaches Can Be Helpful, Why Are They Considered Pests?

Although some people keep roaches for pets, most of us don't want to live with them. Millions of people are allergic to the roach. Cockroach waste and skins that have been shed give these people rashes or make their noses run. Some people have a more severe reaction, such as an **asthma** attack.

Many people believe that roaches are dirty and spread disease. Scientists have found that roaches can pick up germs on their feet. They carry the germs and deposit them somewhere else. So they could spread diseases. There is no proof, however, that this really happens. Because it seems possible, most people prefer to steer clear of cockroaches.

Distancing Humans and Roaches

What is the best way to avoid roaches? Keeping things clean is the best way. Use common sense. Vacuum or sweep floors often. Eat only in the kitchen or dining room. Clean up food that spills. Keep your pets' bowls clean. Don't leave out pet food, or any food, at night. Cover all garbage cans and trash baskets in the kitchen. Keep all food in containers with tight-fitting lids.

Insecticides, agents used to kill insects, can get rid of roaches once they invade. But scientists are trying to find other ways to control these pests. Some hope to learn how to keep roaches from multiplying.

Don't count on getting rid of roaches too soon. If you can't love the roach, try to respect it. It's a mighty tough little bug, and we can learn and benefit a lot from it.

Did You Know *That* About Cockroaches?	
Number of legs on a cockroach	6
Number of knees on most cockroaches	18
Number of minutes cockroaches can hold their breath	40
Percentage of time that cockroaches spend just resting	75
Number of cockroach species worldwide	4,000

Think About the

AFTER READING

Recall

by summarizing the selection in writing or out loud.

My Thinking

The strategy says to recall what I've read by summarizing it in writing or out loud. I can do that by writing or telling the main parts of the selection.

I learned that cockroaches are the most enduring insects and prefer warm temperatures. I thought it was interesting that some cockroaches lay eggs in egg cases, but some clone themselves and don't mate at all. I know now that cockroaches have strong jaws so they can eat anything! Although some cockroaches live indoors, most live outside and don't bother people.

I learned that cockroaches aren't just pests—they are helpful to humans. Scientists learn a lot from them, and they also help plants pollinate and reproduce. I learned a lot about cockroaches from this one article!

Graphic organizers help us organize information we read. I think this article can be organized by using a spider map. Here is how I organized the information. I put my central idea in the middle. I used headings for the legs of the spider. I put details about the headings on the lines coming from the legs.

Spider Map

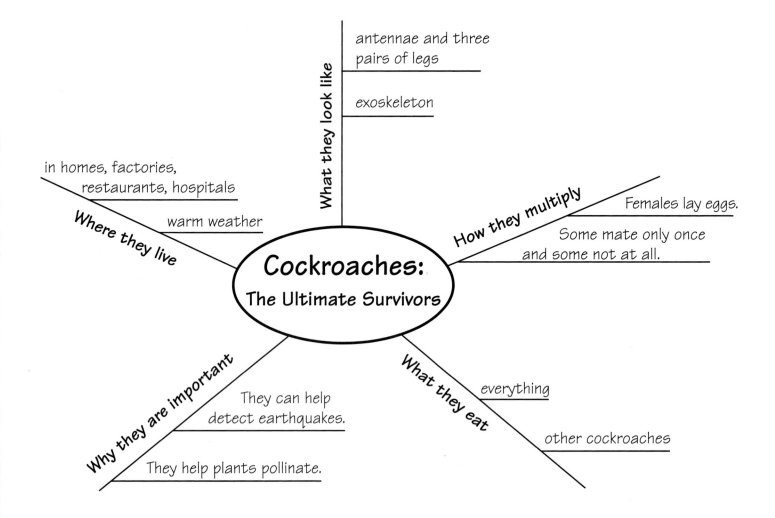

Cockroaches: The Ultimate Survivors

What they look like
- antennae and three pairs of legs
- exoskeleton

How they multiply
- Females lay eggs.
- Some mate only once and some not at all.

Where they live
- in homes, factories, restaurants, hospitals
- warm weather

What they eat
- everything
- other cockroaches

Why they are important
- They can help detect earthquakes.
- They help plants pollinate.

I used my graphic organizer to write a summary of the article. Can you find the information in my summary that came from my map?

A Summary of
Cockroaches: The Ultimate Survivors

Some people might not like cockroaches. They are afraid of what they look like and what they eat. But cockroaches are actually very interesting. And they are also very helpful to people.

Cockroaches like to be warm and cozy, so they stay inside. We might spot them in our homes, factories, restaurants, or hospitals. People can make sure their homes and kitchens are clean to avoid having cockroaches as pets!

Cockroaches have three pairs of jointed legs and long antennae that help them smell. Most roaches have wings, but none has a backbone. These insects have an exoskeleton on the outside that covers and protects their body. The American cockroach can grow to be two inches long. As it gets bigger, it sheds its exoskeleton and grows a bigger one.

Cockroaches are experts at multiplying. Some kinds of female roaches mate just once. That gives them enough sperm to fertilize their eggs for their whole lives. Other kinds of female roaches do not mate at all—they clone themselves. The female roach lays up to 60 eggs in an egg case. After the baby roaches hatch, they do not need Mom's help. They are already able to take care of themselves.

Finding food is not a problem for roaches. They eat everything. They can even live for a whole month without eating. When they get really hungry, they eat each other!

Most people think cockroaches are disgusting, but scientists have found uses for them. For example, roaches can feel small vibrations, such as when the ground shakes slightly just before an earthquake. Someday, these insects might help scientists predict earthquakes. Cockroaches help in another way, too. As they eat, they pick up pollen from one plant and spread it to other plants, allowing the plants to reproduce.

Some people spend a lot of time and money trying to get rid of cockroaches. The best we can do is keep them under control. These tough insects have been on the earth for 350 million years and are here to stay!

Introduction
My introductory paragraph tells readers what they are about to read.

Body
Each paragraph has information from one leg of my spider map. I've written about where cockroaches live, what they look like, how they multiply, what they eat, and why they are important.

Conclusion
I summarized my paper by recalling the main ideas.

Words Adopted From Spanish

Many words in the English language come from the Spanish language. In "Cockroaches: The Ultimate Survivors," you learned that *cockroach* comes from the Spanish word *cucaracha*. People of different cultures met through trade and exploration. Many words from other languages were adopted. Over time, the adopted words changed in spelling and pronunciation.

Here are some more examples of familiar words that come from Spanish:

patio: a terrace or courtyard
siesta: a nap, often taken in the middle of the day
Los Angeles: a city in California founded by Spanish settlers;
At first it was called *La Ciudad de los Angeles* (which means "City of Angels"). Later, people just called it *Los Angeles*.

What other words are adopted from Spanish? Read the following clues and name the words.

1. Name the place in your school where you have lunch. (Hint: from the Spanish word for "coffeehouse")
2. Name a western state in the United States. (Hint: from the Spanish word **montaña,** meaning "mountain")
3. Name an insect that bites to draw blood and leaves an itchy bump. (Hint: three syllables)
4. Name a pack of running animals. (Hint: from the Spanish word for "crash": **estampida**)
5. Name a type of storm that has a funnel of wind. (Hint: from the Spanish **tronada,** meaning "thunderstorm")
6. What is another word for **"slacks"**? (Hint: from the Spanish word **pantalones**)
7. Name the flower that is often sent on Valentine's Day. (Hint: from the Spanish word **rosa**)
8. This is a precious red gem. (Hint: from the Spanish word **rubí**)

Poetry

This poem is about a roach who is thinking about taking a trip. Read this poem several times aloud to yourself until you think you can read it with good expression and rhythm. You may want to read it with a partner, alternating lines or stanzas.

TIP

Poems should be read with a good sense of rhythm. As you practice this poem, try to capture the rhythm in your reading that makes the poem flow.

A Cockroach Takes a Trip

After a meal of cracker crumbs
And the tiniest pieces of cake,
I thought of my cousins from the south
And thought, "That's a trip I might take."

I have known Madagascar roaches
Since first I shed my own skin.
Though I have never met southern cousins,
Even though they are my own kin.

I whistled from my spiracles,
And called with all my might.
Family came out to greet me,
Since it was the middle of night.

"Colombia is not so near,"
said my Great Aunt Louise.
"Your legs will be so tired,
You'll ache in eighteen knees!"

Uncle Fred shook his antennae at me.
He said, "Nephew, have a safe trip.
Those earthquakes down there will keep me here,
at home with some pizza and chips."

Think About
the
Strategies

BEFORE READING

Preview the Selection

by looking at the title and headings to predict what the selection will be about.

 Write notes on your own paper to tell how you used this strategy.

DURING READING

Make Connections

by relating information that I already know about the subject to what I'm reading.

 When you come to a red button like this ⦿, write notes on your own paper to tell how you used this strategy.

DEEP-SEA MONSTER

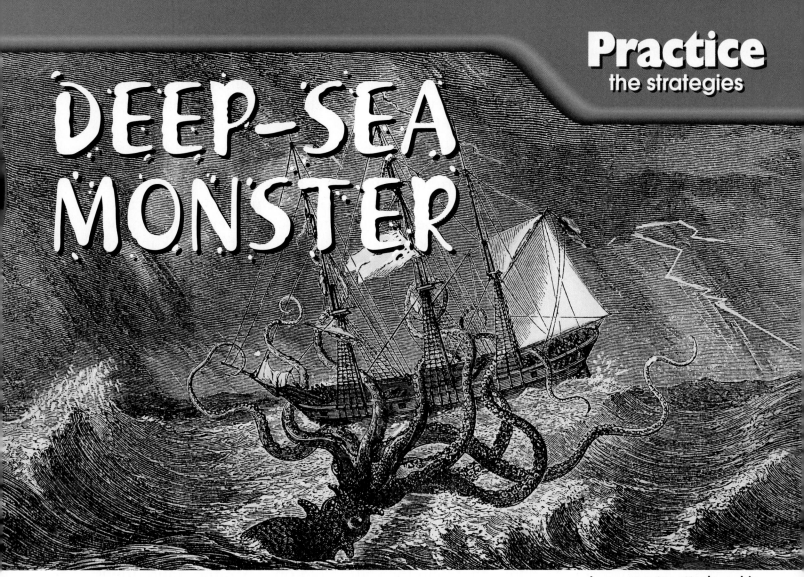

A sea monster attacks a ship in a wood engraving from the 19th century.

Deep down in the darkest depths of the oceans lives a creature that feasts on shark for dinner. It is one of the biggest sea creatures. It lives so deep down that people have seen its natural **habitat** only a few times. What could it be? It's the giant squid! People used to think that the giant squid was an imaginary creature—the subject of tall tales. But this **fascinating** creature is very real indeed.

The Giant Squid's "Family"

Giant squids belong to the group of animals called **mollusks**. These animals have soft bodies and no backbones. Most mollusks have shells. These shells may be inside or outside of the body. Clams, snails, and oysters have shells outside the body. Squids have shells inside their bodies.

Vo•cab•u•lar•y

habitat (hab•i•tat)—the place where something normally lives

fascinating (fas•uh•nay•ting)—very interesting

mollusks (mol•uhsks)—any of a large group of animals that have soft bodies, are without backbones, and usually live in salt water

[25]

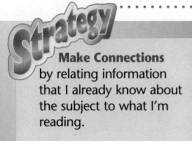
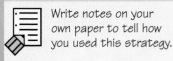
Slugs and octopuses have no shells at all. Although most mollusks live in or next to water, some do not. Snails and slugs live on land.

Giant squids are also **cephalopods**. Cephalopods are mollusks that have large heads, big eyes, and **tentacles**. Tentacles are long, slim parts growing around the mouth or head of some animals. They are used for feeling and gripping. Cuttlefish and octopuses are cephalopods, too. Most cephalopods have a sac that squirts a dark inklike fluid. When a squid squirts its ink into the water, its enemy has a hard time seeing the squid. That makes it easy for the squid to escape.

The Squid's Body

A giant squid can be more than 60 feet long and weigh more than 800 pounds. Look at the diagram of the giant squid. Are you surprised to see both arms *and* tentacles? The squid has 8 arms and 2 tentacles. Compared with the tentacles, the arms are thick and short. Each arm has 2 rows of cup-shaped suckers, parts used for holding things with suction. The tentacles have suckers, too, but just at the ends, on the palms.

When the giant squid hunts, it reaches out with its tentacles to grab its prey. The suckers on the palms have hooks that help the squid hold on. Then the squid draws its prey toward its mouth. The arms grab the prey and bring it to the jaws.

The giant squid has a big head, about 3 feet long. Its mouth is nestled inside the tentacles and arms. The top jaw is pointed. The 2 jaws work together, like a beak, to cut food into pieces. Inside the mouth the radula breaks the food into smaller pieces. Then it pushes the food down into the throat, or **esophagus**. The radula is like a tongue with teeth.

The giant squid has incredibly large eyes. Its eyes can be as big as 10 inches across—larger than the headlights on a car! Because its eyes are so well developed, the giant squid can see very well.

Vo·cab·u·lar·y

cephalopods (**sef**•uh•luh•podz)—mollusks with large heads, large eyes, tentacles, and an ink sac

tentacles (**ten**•tuh•kuhlz)—narrow, flexible parts that certain animals use for feeling, grasping, and moving

esophagus (i•**sof**•uh•guhs)—the tube that connects the throat with the stomach

The Squid's Shell

The giant squid's shell gives the squid its shape and supports its muscles. Its shell is called a pen. The pen is inside the squid's outer covering of muscle called the mantle. The mantle is a pale color on the bottom and becomes brownish or dark red at the top. The squid can change the color of its mantle, depending on how dark the water is or what the squid is doing.

How Giant Squids Breathe

Like a fish, the giant squid breathes through gills. The gills are in its mantle. As the squid moves, water is forced through the two gills so the squid can breathe.

Strategy

Make Connections by relating information that I already know about the subject to what I'm reading.

Write notes on your own paper to tell how you used this strategy.

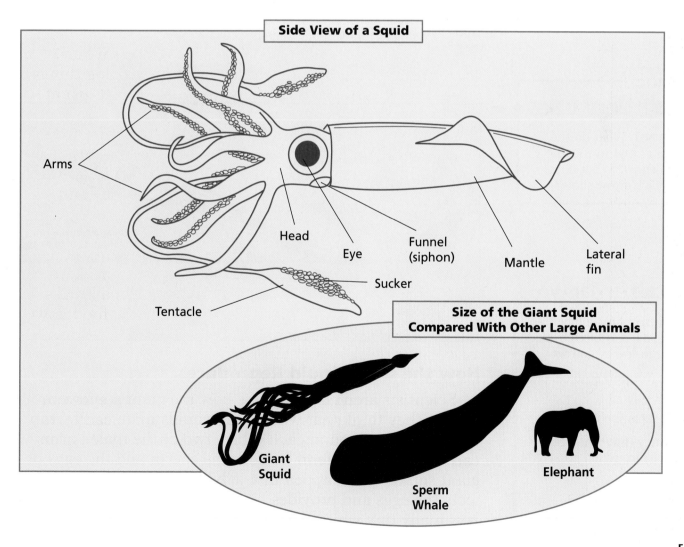

Side View of a Squid

Arms

Head

Eye

Funnel (siphon)

Mantle

Lateral fin

Sucker

Tentacle

Size of the Giant Squid Compared With Other Large Animals

Giant Squid

Sperm Whale

Elephant

A Jet-Propulsion Sea Creature

The squid is jet-propelled. How does it work? To swim forward, the giant squid draws water in through openings between the head and the mantle, then forces the water out through the **siphon,** an organ that **expels** water. This shoots the squid forward. To change direction, the squid moves its fins. The fins also help keep the squid **stable.** Squids swim quickly and gracefully, so they easily catch their prey.

The giant squid can move up and down. It does this by changing its **buoyancy.** Buoyancy is the ability to float. Because the giant squid is heavy, it needs to change its buoyancy to avoid sinking. How does it do that? For a squid, it's easy. Its muscles contain **ammonium** ions. These tiny particles make the squid light. When the squid's muscles have a lot of these ions, the squid can rise in the water. As the squid releases some of the ions, it becomes heavier, allowing it to sink.

Using Text Features

Diagram What do the white arrows in the diagram show? What does the black arrow show?

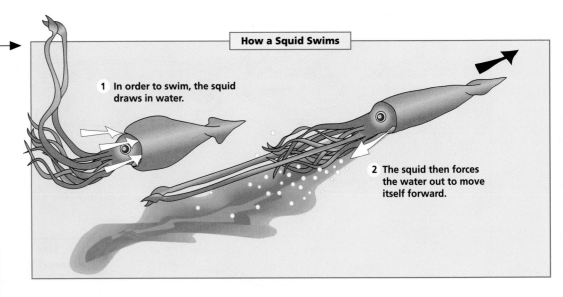

How a Squid Swims

1 In order to swim, the squid draws in water.

2 The squid then forces the water out to move itself forward.

Vo•cab•u•lar•y

siphon (**sy**•fuhn)—a tube filled with liquid that is forced by air pressure to flow up and out

expels (ik•**spelz**)—forces or drives out

stable (**stay**•buhl)—steady

buoyancy (**boy**•uhn•see)— the ability to remain afloat

ammonium (uh•**moh**•nee•uhm)— a chemical ion

How the Giant Squid Reproduces

Scientists aren't exactly sure how the giant squid reproduces. They think that when giant squids mate, they wrap their tentacles around each other. Two of the male's arms carry sperm to the female. Both the sperm and the eggs of giant squids are wrapped in a jellylike substance. This protects the eggs and provides food for them. The female then lays many tiny white eggs that float in the water.

When the young squids come out of the eggs, they are well developed. They look like small adult squids. At first, the young squid stays attached to the egg. The food in the egg continues to **nourish** the young squid until it is old enough to find its own food.

Living in the Abyssal Region

Giant squids live deep in the waters of the Atlantic and Pacific oceans. In their home territory, the water is probably between 1,640 and 4,900 feet deep. This part of the ocean that is home to the giant squids is called the **abyssal**

region. Most of the region is a flat ocean plain, but there are some volcanic mountain peaks. Some peaks are tall enough to break the surface of the water. The abyssal region has very cold water, no light, and strong water pressure. About 85 percent of all the oceans in the world are made up of this deep-sea **environment**. It is the largest environment in the world.

Squid feeding on prey

Similar to a desert on land, this region has few forms of plant and animal life. Few living forms can survive here. Because there aren't many creatures, some of the creatures here grow to be quite large. All of the animals that live here are **predators**. Like the giant squid, these fish—such as dragonfish, knifefish, hatchet fish, and sea devils—hunt live prey. They also eat the bodies of other animals that have drifted to the bottom of the ocean.

The giant squid almost never comes to the surface of the ocean on its own. In 2004, researchers in Japan used an underwater camera to take pictures of a living giant squid. But humans have rarely seen a giant squid in its habitat. Mostly, we have learned about the giant squid by studying dead ones caught in fishing nets or washed up onshore.

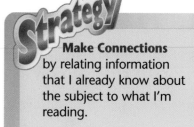

Make Connections by relating information that I already know about the subject to what I'm reading.

Write notes on your own paper to tell how you used this strategy.

Vo·cab·u·lar·y

nourish (**nur**•ish)—to feed

abyssal (uh•**bis**•uhl)—great depths of the ocean

environment (en•**vy**•ruhn•muhnt)— surroundings

predators (**pred**•uh•tuhrz)— animals that live by hunting and eating other animals

The Giant Squid's Mortal Enemy

Does the giant squid have an enemy? Could a creature this huge actually have an enemy? Yes. The giant squid and the sperm whale are fierce enemies.

Whales live at the ocean's surface. They are **mammals** and need to breathe air. Whales are excellent divers, and they dive to capture food. The sperm whale, in fact, is able to dive at least a mile (5,280 feet) down. This takes it into the giant squid's home waters.

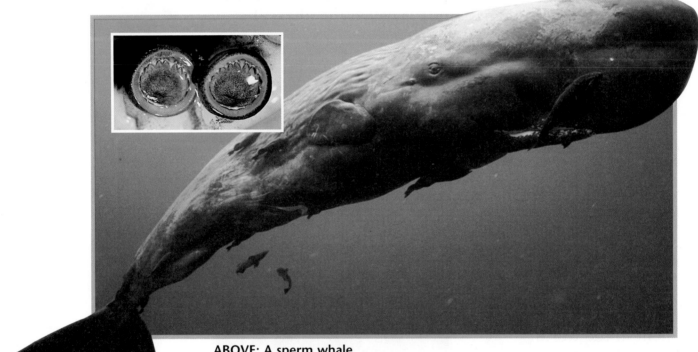

ABOVE: A sperm whale
INSET: The suckers of a giant squid are lined with razor-sharp teeth. Suckers like these have left scars on sperm whales.

Sperm whales have huge mouths and powerful jaws. Giant squids have long tentacles and strong arms with powerful suckers. When these foes meet, the squid wraps its tentacles around the whale and holds it tight with its arms. If the whale cannot grab onto the squid with its jaws to kill it, the squid holds the whale underwater until the whale drowns.

Scientists have learned how large giant squids can grow by studying the scars around the mouths of sperm whales. A 50-foot squid has suckers that leave a 4-inch scar. Scientists have found sucker scars that are 18 inches across. They think that the giant squid that left these scars may have been more than 200 feet long!

Vo·**cab**·u·lar·y

mammals (**mam**•uhlz)— animals whose females produce milk to feed their young

Why Giant Squids Are Important

Giant squids are important. They are a **vital** link in the ocean food chain. The food chain is a connection among plants and animals in which each living thing feeds upon the one below it and is eaten by the one above it. At the bottom of the chain are **microplankton**. These tiny, plant-like organisms float, often at the surface of the ocean. Like plants, microplankton use the sun's energy and nutrients from the water to grow. Microplankton are food for animal **microorganisms**. These are animals so small that you can see them only with a microscope. Fish eat animal microorganisms. Giant squids eat fish. Next in line in the chain is the sperm whale, whose prime food is squid.

Does anything eat the sperm whale? Until 2003, scientists did not believe so. However, in that year, the largest squid to date was discovered. Called the colossal squid, it is even larger than the giant squid. Its prey—sperm whales.

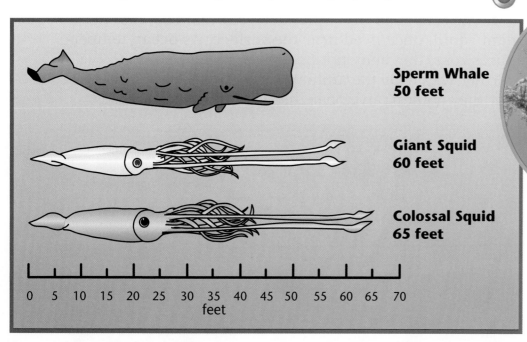

**Sperm Whale
50 feet**

**Giant Squid
60 feet**

**Colossal Squid
65 feet**

0 5 10 15 20 25 30 35 40 45 50 55 60 65 70
feet

Marine microplankton greatly magnified

What Scientists Have Learned by Studying the Giant Squids

Scientists have learned much about the giant squid. The giant squid, for instance, has keen eyesight and sees well in very dark water. This is because its eyes have a lot of cells that "catch" light. In fact, some cephalopods have twice the number of light-catching cells that humans have. In the same amount of light, it is believed that squids

Vo·cab·u·lar·y

vital (**vyt**•l)—necessary to life

microplankton (**my**•kroh•**plangk**•tuhn)—tiny plantlike organisms on the surface of the ocean

microorganisms (my•kroh•**or**•guh•niz•uhmz)—living things so small they can only be seen by using a microscope

[31]

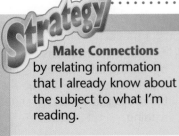
Make Connections
by relating information
that I already know about
the subject to what I'm
reading.

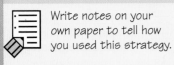

Write notes on your
own paper to tell how
you used this strategy.

could see better than humans. They may be able to see details of objects that people could not see at all. All squids also have well-developed brains and complex nervous systems. These help them move and behave in complicated ways. The huge size of the giant squid makes it especially interesting to scientists.

How the Giant Squid Evolved

We don't know how or why this ocean giant developed as it did. Scientists do know that the squid and the octopus have been around for at least 200 million years. Many cephalopods existed long before that; some no longer exist. The earliest cephalopods, such as the nautilus, had external shells. Some had shells that were 3 feet across. Today, the nautilus is the only one from this group of cephalopods that has survived.

Some scientists think that deep-sea animals, like the giant squid, once lived near the surface. As ocean temperatures rose, they may not have been able to adapt to the warmer water. Or the animals may have changed so much that they couldn't live near the surface. In either case,

This nautilus is a cephalopod.

they moved deeper in order to survive. However, since the discovery of the colossal squid, we now know that some squid can move up to the surface and live. Many more facts about giant and colossal squids are yet to be found.

Answers in the Ocean

Giant squids, colossal squids, sperm whales, and other giant creatures have survived for a long time. Long before the earliest recorded sightings of giant and colossal squids, people told stories of deep-sea monsters. Tales were told of long arms wrapping around the masts of sailing ships or dragging sailors into the sea. Many of the descriptions sound like a huge squid or octopus. Do you think that these stories were about giant or colossal squids, or do you think there might be other bigger deep-sea monsters waiting to be discovered? The depths of the ocean hide the answer—for now. Maybe you will someday be part of a scientific team investigating the latest deep-sea discovery!

Think About the Strategy

AFTER READING

Recall by summarizing the selection in writing or out loud.

Write notes on your own paper to tell how you used this strategy.

Root Words

Many words in English come from Greek or Latin roots. **Root words** are words that you can make new words from by adding prefixes or suffixes. The root word can also stand on its own as a word. Knowing the meaning of a root can help you determine the meaning of new words.

Look at the word *buoyancy* in the following passage from "Deep-Sea Monster":

> *The giant squid can move up and down. It does this by changing its* **buoyancy**.

Buoyancy's root is the word *buoy*, which means "to float." Have you heard of the word *buoy*? A buoy is a floating object that is anchored in the water as a marker. You may have seen a buoy in a lake or the ocean.

Look at the following sentence. It uses another word with the root *buoy*. Use your knowledge of *buoy* to figure out what the word means.

> Luckily, my prize from the carnival was **buoyant,** or else I wouldn't have found it after my sister threw it in the pool.

The root **aqua** means "water." Use the meaning of this root and how the word is used in the sentence to write a definition for each of the following boldfaced words.

1. My parents bought me an **aquarium** and three freshwater rainbow fish for my birthday.
2. The **aquanaut** collected information on great white sharks for the research team.
3. **Aquatic** sports include water polo, synchronized swimming, and diving.
4. My birthday is in March, so I have an **aquamarine** ring.
5. We enjoyed watching the swimmers and divers perform at the **aquacade.**

Log

Practice reading this log until you can read it with appropriate expression and phrasing. Important information is being communicated in the log. Read this with a slower, strong voice.

As you read this log, imagine yourself as the writer. Try to use your voice to express the excitement of the writer. Be sure to pause slightly at the commas. This will help the listener to better understand the reading.

Ship's Log—Submarine Hound Dog

Our Mission: Track sperm whale and observe feeding habits

January 20, 10:02 AM, 2,400 feet below surface
We spot our first sperm whale motoring along looking for prey. We nickname her "Eve."

January 22, 2:34 PM, 3,000 feet below surface

We haven't seen Eve since yesterday. Joan, our biologist, has just sighted a male shark finishing lunch. We nickname him "Adam."

January 22, 2:46 PM, 3,100 feet below surface

A smoky, giant cloud suddenly appears in our window, which Joan says is ink from the giant squid we call "Mr. Pepper." He doesn't look happy about Adam, who wants to make a snack out of him.

January 22, 3:36 PM, 3,200 feet below surface

The ink has cleared, and the battle is on! It's a fight between a shark and a squid with a head over 3 feet long. The total length of Mr. Pepper looks to be 60 feet or more! Oh, no, the squid has one of its tentacles wrapped around Adam. Maybe it's Mr. Pepper who will have shark for dinner.

January 22, 3:59 PM, 3,000 feet below surface

Adam broke free and swam away. That fight was some entertainment down in this abyssal region of the ocean. Mr. Pepper must be hiding, so we decide to leave our cephalopod pal alone. We don't want to become Mr. Pepper's next meal!

Think About the
Strategies

BEFORE READING

Preview the Selection
by looking at the title and headings to predict what the selection will be about.

DURING READING

Make Connections
by relating information that I already know about the subject to what I'm reading.

AFTER READING

Recall
by summarizing the selection in writing or out loud.

 Use your own paper to jot notes to apply these Before, During, and After Reading Strategies. In this selection, you will choose when to stop, think, and respond.

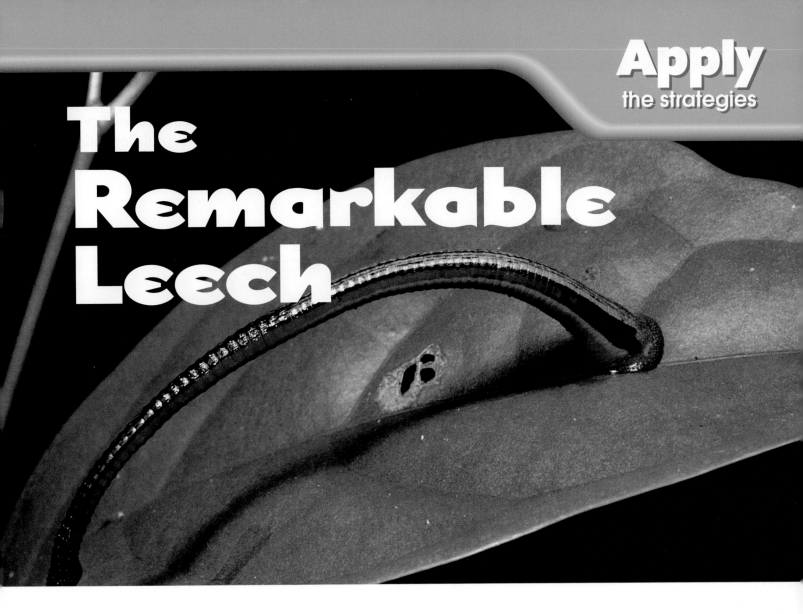

The Remarkable Leech

In 1799, an army led by the French general Napoleon Bonaparte was marching from Egypt to Syria. Along the way, many soldiers began to die in strange ways. Some men **suffocated**. Some men mysteriously bled to death— but they had no wounds. Why were they dying?

The Answer

The desert heat was strong. The thirsty men drank from every water source they could find. They did not know that tiny leeches lived in many of the water holes. When the men drank, they swallowed leeches along with the water. The leeches attached themselves to the inside of the soldiers' mouths and throats. Some entered the men's lungs.

Vo·cab·u·lar·y

suffocated (suf•uh•kay•tid)
—died from lack of oxygen

[37]

Then, the leeches began drinking their blood! As the leeches drank the men's blood, the leeches' bodies swelled. The tiny leeches grew larger and larger. They blocked the soldiers' air passages, and the men couldn't breathe. Soldiers who had swallowed too many leeches died from loss of blood.

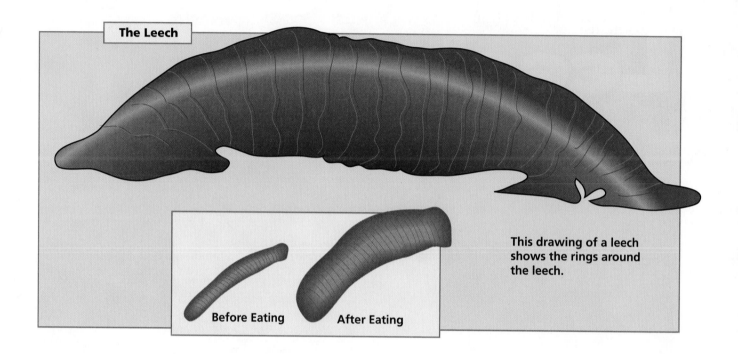

The Leech

This drawing of a leech shows the rings around the leech.

Before Eating

After Eating

What Is a Leech?

If you have ever waded in a stream and come out with leeches stuck to your toes and ankles, you know what a leech looks like. But just what is a leech?

A leech is a kind of worm. Its body is divided into 34 circular sections, or rings. At one end of the leech is a small sucker—like a suction cup—that contains the leech's mouth. In some types of leech, the mouth has 3 teeth. The leech uses these teeth to break through the skin of its prey. At the other end of the leech is a second, larger sucker. The leech uses this sucker to hold on to surfaces.

There are about 300 different **species,** or types, of leech. Most leeches are **parasites**. They stick to other animals and live by feeding on their blood. Some species of leech eat **decayed** plant matter. Others eat smaller animals, such as snails and worms.

Vo·cab·u·lar·y

species (spee•sheez)— a group of animals or plants that are similar and are able to mate and have offspring

parasites (par•uh•sytz)— organisms that live and feed on other organisms

decayed (di•kayd)—rotten

Leeches range in size from 1/4 inch to 18 inches long. Most leeches are 1 to 2 inches long. As a leech moves, it stretches its body into a thin, snakelike shape. By stretching, the leech seems to be much longer than it really is. A leech can eat 10 times its weight in blood. As a leech sucks its prey's blood, its body swells. A leech can double or triple its size in minutes.

Some leeches are a dull greenish brown. Others are black. Still others have lines of spots down their backs. Some are even bright with red, orange, or yellow stripes.

Where Leeches Live

Many leeches are tropical animals that live in jungles and swamps. However, leeches are found all over the world in all types of climates. They live in desert water holes and on mountains. Strange as this may sound, there are more leeches living in Antarctic waters than in all the tropics.

Most leeches are **aquatic**. They live in freshwater ponds and streams. A few species are found in both saltwater and freshwater environments. Aquatic leeches can swim.

A pond leech

Vo·cab·u·lar·y

aquatic (uh•**kwat**•ik)—living in or on the water

Both aquatic and land leeches expand and **contract** their muscles in order to move. Some can use their suckers to move. They attach one sucker to an object, then flip over to attach the other sucker. The motion is similar to a giant metal spring going end over end down stairs.

Land leeches live in hot, damp parts of the world. They wait for their prey in wet plants and under decaying leaves. Soldiers in Vietnam reported that in the jungle, leeches dropped from the trees like rain. The soldiers had to cover all parts of their bodies. Still, leeches were able to get inside their clothing. Small leeches have been known to squeeze through the lace holes of hiking boots!

Are leeches anything but pests? You'd be surprised!

Leeches in Early Medicine

Long ago, doctors thought that many diseases could be cured by bloodletting. This means draining people's blood. The Egyptians, Aztecs, and other ancient peoples practiced bloodletting. For a long time, doctors thought that bloodletting could cure many ills. They used it for mental illness, skin disease, and fever, among other things.

This 17th century illustration shows a young doctor bleeding a wealthy woman as her servants stand by.

Vo·**cab**·u·lar·y

contract (kuhn•**trakt**)— to make smaller by drawing together

[40]

In the 18th and 19th centuries, doctors used leeches to treat headaches. They stuck leeches to the sides of the forehead and let them draw blood! For many reasons, doctors liked to use leeches instead of cutting patients with knives. Leeches were easy to find—they lived in marshes, ponds, and streams all across Europe. They also stuck themselves to human skin without causing pain. The doctors could control how much blood a leech sucked. Best of all, patients didn't worry about cuts or lasting scars.

As we now know, losing blood doesn't cure disease. It just makes people weaker and sicker. By the late 1800s, science won out. Better methods and medicines were found. Bloodletting was no longer seen as a cure for everything.

The Worm Returns

Leeches are now making a comeback! This does not mean a return to bloodletting. Instead, doctors have come to see just how remarkable leeches are.

Surgeons can now reattach fingers, ears, and other body parts that have been cut off. However, there are often problems with tiny veins that the surgeons can't reconnect. Fresh blood flows into the reattached body part but has no way to leave it. Blood can collect in pools in that body part. This can cause swelling, pain, and the death of the body part. Doctors use leeches to drain off the extra blood. When the leech is full of blood, it just drops off.

The procedure is nearly pain-free. Leeches have an **anesthetic**—a painkiller—in their saliva. Leech saliva also contains an **anticoagulant;** it keeps blood from clotting. After the leech drops off, the wound it creates keeps bleeding for several hours. This helps keep the swelling down.

Leeches to the Rescue

In 1985, a boy was brought to a hospital after being bitten by a dog. The dog had bitten off the boy's ear. Surgeons sewed the ear back on. However, clots began forming in the boy's veins. The doctors tried anticoagulants, but that did not solve the problem. Although blood

A leech after sucking blood for an hour

Vo•**cab**•u•lar•y

anesthetic (an•is•**thet**•ik)— a drug that causes loss of feeling or consciousness in order to block pain

anticoagulant (an•tee•koh•**ag**•yuh•luhnt)— a substance that prevents clotting of blood

was flowing to the boy's ear, it could not get from his ear back to his heart. Doctors then stuck leeches onto the boy's ear every few hours. He called them his "tickle friends" and gave them names like Fred and Chubby. The leeches got the blood flowing. After a week, the boy went home with his ear safely attached.

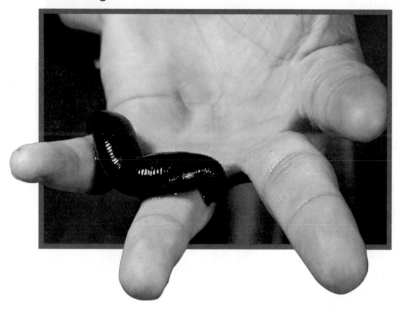

A leech sucking blood from a finger

A factory worker in England caught his long hair in a machine. It tore off his scalp. After surgeons reattached the scalp, they applied leeches to help the blood flow. The treatment was a success.

In another case, a woman had caught her fingers in a power saw. One finger was cut off, and three others were badly hurt. Surgeons reattached the **severed** finger. However, it began to turn black as clots formed in the veins. At first, the surgeons were afraid they would have to remove the finger. Instead, they used leeches to drain off the blood. The woman's finger was saved.

How do patients feel about being treated with leeches? At first, most people are scared. Few people enjoy the idea of having a leech suck their blood! When they see that the treatment works, though, they change their minds.

Today, leeches are used in many medical procedures. The worm has returned!

A Chemical Resource

Scientists have learned that leeches make several useful chemicals. Anticoagulants are just some of these. Some chemicals produced by leeches are used to treat blood disorders and severe bruises.

Another important chemical in leech saliva digests the "cement" that holds cells together. Separating the cells lets the leech saliva spread deeper than it normally would. This increases the flow of blood to the leech. Doctors use this chemical to speed the delivery of some drugs and anesthetics.

Vo·cab·u·lar·y

severed (sev•uhrd)—to have become cut off or detached

Scientists are studying many other substances that leeches make. Leeches can safely store the blood they drink for months. An **antibiotic** the leech produces keeps the blood from spoiling. A strong antibiotic such as this can have many uses in people. Another substance in the leech makes blood vessels bigger. This may be useful in treating bad headaches.

Helpful Tool in Fighting Cancer

Scientists studying lung cancer found that a substance in leech saliva can stop the cancer from spreading. This same substance can also reduce the side effects of some cancer drugs.

Some scientists think leeches will be used in the fight against heart attacks and strokes. Leeches may even be used to treat eye diseases that can lead to blindness.

What other wonders may come from research into leeches? Some researchers think that their studies of leech nerve cells will explain how damaged nerve cells regrow. They hope that their studies will show how nerves are formed and how they work.

New Life for Leeches

The need for leeches in the 1800s nearly led to their dying out. In 1863 alone, hospitals in London, England, used more than seven million leeches! The new interest in leeches may threaten this animal that is disappearing from the wild.

By the late 1980s, leeches were becoming hard to find in Europe. Scientists had collected too many. Another reason leeches were disappearing was that the wetlands where leeches lived were being drained. No one really knows whether the medicinal leech is in danger. However, collecting leeches in the wild no longer fills the need.

Breeding leeches has become one way to meet the demand and save the species. In 1983, Biopharm, a Welsh company, began raising leeches for medicine. Today, it sells live leeches and the chemicals they make to countries around the world. Meanwhile, in the wild, leeches are free to recover.

Leeches can be annoying creatures. But they can also be important medical tools. Because they are so useful, it looks as if people are "stuck on" leeches!

Scientists are now breeding leeches. These leeches are shown with their eggs.

Vo•cab•u•lar•y

antibiotic (an•ti•by•ot•ik)— a substance that can stop the growth of germs

Multiple Meanings

One word can mean many things. You can find out which meaning the author intends by how the word is used in the sentence. For example, the word *contract* has three meanings:

a. (noun) an agreement, especially a written one
b. (verb) to make smaller
c. (verb) to obtain or to get something like an illness

The word *contract* is used in "The Remarkable Leech" in the following way. Which of the three meanings above makes sense in this sentence?

*Aquatic leeches can **contract** their muscles in order to move.*

The sentence is about how the leeches work their muscles in order to move. Therefore, *contract* means "to make smaller."

Read the following sentences. Decide which meaning of the word *contract* is most suitable for the way it is used in each sentence. Write **a, b,** or **c** on a separate piece of paper.

1. When you inhale, your lungs expand, and when you exhale, your lungs **contract**.
2. Nicole told me that you can **contract** chickenpox from chickens, but I don't believe her.
3. Juan Diaz just signed a five-year **contract** with the Philadelphia Falcons.
4. Fewer people today **contract** smallpox because of immunizations.
5. The **contract** stated that we could move into the new house by next Friday.

Readers' Theater

In "The Remarkable Leech" you just read about how leeches killed Napoleon Bonaparte's soldiers. Read this script about how that might have happened. As you read, make your voice reflect the worry and fear Napoleon and his troops were facing.

Fluency **TIP**

Remember that exclamation marks indicate that a word or phrase should be read with greater emphasis and enthusiasm than other words.

The March Between Egypt and Syria

Narrator: November 9, 1799. This desert is a long way from Paris. There's nothing here but sand and sun.

Napoleon: It's a rough march through this spitting hot country. It's low on water, and there's no river in sight. My men won't make it if we don't find a river soon. We'll all die. Without water, there's nothing ahead but death!

Lieutenant Larpenteur: Sir! Just ahead—look! A stream.

Napoleon: A stream? It's more like a series of ditches. This water's filthy, but my men are on their knees drinking straight from the source.

Narrator: November 12, 1799. Dirty water is better than no water at all. Napoleon orders his men to fill buckets and canteens with water from the streams before moving on. On November 17, 1799, army doctor Simonet comes to Napoleon with trouble on his mind.

Doctor Simonet: Bad news, General, sir! Yesterday the cook died. Today, three more men suffocated—for no reason that I can see. Yes, the desert lacks water, but there's plenty of air. How can four men die in the middle of such wide open spaces?

Narrator: November 19, 1799. Lieutenant Larpenteur counts the dead.

Lieutenant Larpenteur: The tragedy continues, sir. Six men died yesterday. Three more men died today. And four men are bleeding inside their bodies!

Doctor Simonet: Drink lots of water, men. That's an order. There are more streams, so we have a good supply of water now. This dry air has to be the killer. So drink more water!

Napoleon: Even without a battle, my men keep dying around me. Who or what is this invisible enemy?

Steps in a Process

How A Cockroach Becomes a Fossil

You may have seen a dinosaur fossil, but have you ever seen a cockroach fossil? Most fossils are animals that had bones or hard shells. Few are insects. Yet sometimes insects, like cockroaches, are preserved. In 2001, scientists from the Ohio State University found the world's largest cockroach fossil. It was discovered in a coal mine in eastern Ohio. This cockroach was three and one-half inches long. That's twice as long as most American roaches. Some roaches that now live in the tropics are 4 inches long. Still, this is the biggest cockroach fossil ever found. Now this huge insect is helping us learn about ancient life.

How did this cockroach become a fossil? Long ago, eastern Ohio was a tropical swamp. Many plants, animals, and insects lived there. Here's how this cockroach became a fossil:

1. After the cockroach died, its body sank into the mud and was quickly buried.

2. Mud seeped into the cockroach's body. The mud somehow kept it from decaying.

3. Over time, minerals from the mud replaced parts of the cockroach's body.

4. As the minerals hardened into rock, they kept the exact shape of the cockroach.

5. Millions of years later, workers digging coal in the mine found the cockroach fossil.

Discussion Questions

Answer these questions with a partner or on a separate sheet of paper.

1. How long is this cockroach fossil, compared to American roaches today?

2. What happened after the dead cockroach became buried in the mud?
   a. The miners found it.
   b. Minerals took the place of parts of its body.
   c. The minerals turned into mud.
   d. The cockroach's body turned into mud.

3. Which step was not essential for the cockroach to become a fossil?
   a. Mud seeped into the cockroach's body. The mud somehow kept it from decaying.
   b. Over time, minerals from the mud replaced parts of the cockroach's body.
   c. As the minerals hardened into rock, they kept the exact shape of the cockroach.
   d. Millions of years later, workers digging coal in the mine found the cockroach fossil.

4. Why is the fossil in the same shape as the cockroach?
   a. Minerals from the mud replaced parts of the cockroach's body.
   b. Rock formed around the cockroach's body.
   c. Seeping water carved the rock into the shape of the cockroach.
   d. The fossil is the cockroach's body.

5. What is more important about this cockroach fossil, its age or its size?

6. Which statement below is probably accurate?
   a. The giant cockroach was the only fossil in the coal mine.
   b. The scientists found some cockroach fossils that were even bigger.
   c. The scientists found some cockroach fossils that were smaller.
   d. The cockroach looked exactly like American roaches today.

7. Will scientists ever find the largest cockroach that lived in ancient times?

8. Which is more likely to become a fossil, a cockroach or a turtle? Why?

EXPLORE MORE

Present a Radio Announcement

Present a radio story on each of the creatures in this unit: the cockroach, the giant squid, and the leech. Be sure to give background information on each and explain to the listeners why each of these creatures is important to humankind.

Present a Report

Present a report from under the sea. Describe your surroundings and the giant and colossal squids you encounter while you are observing. Use sound effects, if you like. Show drawings or photographs of the creatures you describe.

Make a Book

Work in a small group to make an illustrated book about unusual cockroaches that live around the world. Provide a map showing where each type lives.

Write a Report

Write a report on the creatures that coexist with the giant squid in the abyssal region of the ocean. Tell about how they relate (or don't relate) to each other. Use a graphic or other visuals to explain some relationships.

Write a Newspaper Article

Write a newspaper article about the woman whose fingers were cut off by a power saw. Include background information about how leeches have been used in medicine throughout history.

Present a Newscast

Work in a small group to present a newscast about leeches. Include two or three stories about how people have been helped by leeches.

Related Books

Clarke, Penny. *Spiders, Insects, and Minibeasts*. Franklin Watts, 2003.

Dussling, Jennifer. *Giant Squid: Mystery of the Deep*. Grosset & Dunlap, 1999.

Ellis, Richard. *The Search for the Giant Squid*. The Lyons Press, 1998.

Garcia, Eulalia. *Giant Squid: Monsters of the Deep*. Gareth Stevens, 1997.

Merrick, Patrick. *Cockroaches*. The Child's World, Inc., 2003.

—*Leeches*. The Child's World, Inc., 2003.

Parker, Janice. *Cockroaches, Cocoons, and Honeycombs: The Science of Insects*. Raintree Steck-Vaughn, 2000.

Redmond, Shirley Raye. *Tentacles! Tales of the Giant Squid*. Random House, 2003.

Schaefer, Lola M. *Leeches*. Heinemann Library, 2002.

Stone, Lynn M. *What Makes an Insect?* The Rourke Book Co. Inc., 1997.

Wechsler, Doug. *Bizarre Birds*. Boyds Mills Press, 1999.

Woods, Samuel G. *Sorting Out Worms and Other Invertebrates: Everything You Want to Know About Insects, Corals, Mollusks, Sponges, and More!* Blackbirch Press, 1999.

Interesting Web Sites

Cockroaches

http://www.bio.umass.edu/biology/kunkel/cockroach_faq.html

http://www.abc.net.au/science/news/stories/s409585.htm

http://yucky.kids.discovery.com/noflash/roaches/index.html

http://www.conceptlab.com/roachbot

Squids

http://seawifs.gsfc.nasa.gov/squid.html

http://www.unmuseum.mus.pa.us/squid.htm

http://nationalgeographic.com/news/2005/09/0927_giant_squid.html

Leeches

http://www.accessexcellence.org/LC/SS/leechlove.html

http://www.leeches.biz/about-leeches.htm

http://www.biokids.umich.edu/critters/annelida

Web sites have been carefully researched for accuracy, content, and appropriateness. However, teachers and caregivers are reminded that Web sites are subject to change. Internet use should always be monitored.

Activate Prior Knowledge

by looking at the title, headings, pictures, and graphics to decide what I know about this topic.

Interact With Text

by identifying the main idea and supporting details.

Evaluate

by searching the selection to determine how the author used evidence to reach conclusions.

LEARN
the strategies
in the selection
Archaeologists—History's Detectives
page 53

PRACTICE
the *strategies*
in the selection
Ancient Timekeepers
page 67

APPLY
the *strategies*
in the selection
Cracking the Code of Hammurabi
page 79

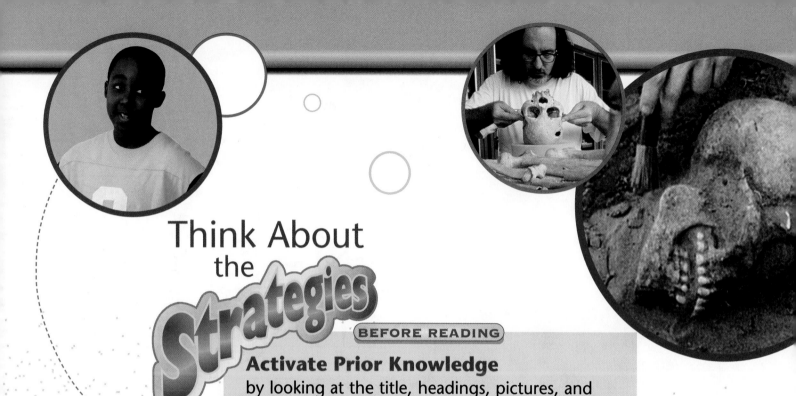

Think About
the
Strategies

Activate Prior Knowledge

by looking at the title, headings, pictures, and graphics to decide what I know about this topic.

My Thinking

This strategy says to activate prior knowledge by looking at the title, headings, pictures, and graphics to decide what I know about this topic. The title tells me that I am going to read about archaeologists. I also see a picture of someone digging up bones. I have read other stories about archaeologists going on digs.

The headings suggest that I will be reading about how archaeologists go about doing their work. So I will probably read more about the digs that they go on.

I also see maps and charts. I remember seeing a news report on television about archaeologists working in Africa. Maybe I will find out more about that as I read this selection.

DURING READING

Interact With Text

by identifying the main idea and supporting details.

My Thinking

This strategy says to interact with text by identifying the main ideas and supporting details. I will stop and think about this strategy every time I come to a red button like this ⦿.

Archaeologists— History's Detectives

Did you ever go to a museum and look at a statue? Did you wonder how people knew it was 5,000 years old? Did you wonder how they found it? Have you ever wanted to know how someone your age lived 10,000 years ago?

There are people who spend much of their lives answering these kinds of questions. They are called archaeologists. These scientists study objects and structures to learn about the past. Archaeologists are like detectives. They search for clues to life thousands of years ago. They tell us how people lived in the past.

Archaeologists search for objects in the ground, in riverbeds, in ice, on mountains, and under the ocean. They look for **artifacts, ecofacts,** and **features** that help them

Vo·cab·u·lar·y

artifacts (ar·tuh·fakts)— objects made by humans

ecofacts (ek·oh·fakts)— objects brought to a place but not made by humans, such as stones or shells

features (fee·chuhrz)— artifacts that can't be moved, such as walls or pyramids

Strategy

Interact With Text by identifying the main idea and supporting details.

My Thinking

The heading asks, "How Do Archaeologists Work?" This section answers that question. That's the main idea.

Some of the supporting details are:

• Start with a hypothesis.

• Make a plan.

• Collect and analyze data from lots of places.

Vo•cab•u•lar•y

hypothesis (hy•**poth**•i•sis)— a possible explanation for an observation or problem that can be tested

sifter (**sift**•uhr)— an instrument for separating large pieces from tiny ones

tell a story. They find pieces of stone, bone, tools, pottery, food, and buildings. After finding these clues, they put them together like a giant puzzle. They then use this puzzle to weave a story of ancient worlds.

How Do Archaeologists Work?

All good scientists find answers to questions. Archaeologists do the same thing. Much as you do in science class, they start with a problem or an idea. Then they make a **hypothesis**—an idea or answer—that they assume is true. Then they set out to prove whether the hypothesis is right or wrong. They make a plan, collect data (facts and figures), analyze the data, come to conclusions, and then tell others about it. The results of their work tell us much about life on the earth thousands of years ago.

Archaeologists work hard. They spend weeks in caves, deserts, and ice fields. Some work in swamps, in jungles, and under the sea. Others work in huge old buildings, underneath busy cities, and in many other places.

Archaeologists spend hours digging with tiny shovels and using toothbrushes to brush away dust and dirt. They sift through tons of dirt and pick out tiny objects. Each object is a clue. Each object must be recorded (or written about), studied, and tested. Some archaeologists spend all their time in the laboratory. Most days nothing is found. But when they do find something—whether in the field, in a **sifter,** or in the laboratory—they are really excited!

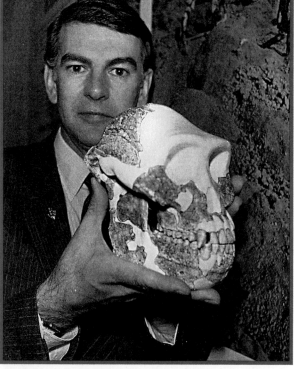

Dr. Donald Johanson holding a replica of a 3-million-year-old skull

Making a Plan

The work might start in a professor's office or in a library. Sometimes it begins in a field somewhere.

This was the case for Donald Johanson, an **anthropologist,** and a group of archaeologists. In 1971, they had found stone tools and fossils in Africa—in a place called Hadar, Ethiopia. Someone had made these tools a very long time ago.

Could the earliest people on Earth have come from this place? To test this hypothesis, the group decided to plan another trip. First, they made a research plan. The plan told how they would go about confirming their hypothesis. They needed to find money to pay for the trip and people to help them. Once they had money and people, they were ready to start!

Searching for Data

The objects that archaeologists seek are found in all kinds of places, even buildings. Some ancient buildings, such as the pyramids in Egypt and those on the Acropolis (uh•**krop**•uh•lis) in Greece, are still standing. Archaeologists study them to try to learn how people lived

Archaeologists and anthropologists found ancient stone tools and fossils in Africa.

Using
Text Features

Map The large map shows an area with many sites where archaeologists have found stone tools and fossils. What does the inset map show?

Answer: The inset map shows the location of the area on the continent of Africa.

The Parthenon (top right) and the Temple of Athena Nike (lower left) on the Acropolis in Athens, Greece

Vo•**cab**•u•lar•y

anthropologist
(an•thruh•**pol**•uh•jist)—
a scientist who studies human beings

[55]

Strategy

Interact With Text by identifying the main idea and supporting details.

My Thinking

I think the main idea of this section is Searching for Data, just like the heading.

This section tells about how archaeologists find objects. Here are the details that explain this:

- They look in fields, deserts, caves—all kinds of places.
- Sometimes they dig in the ground.
- They look for clues, study maps, and do surveys.

Vo·cab·u·lar·y

excavate (ek•skuh•vayt)—to uncover by digging; to dig out

surveys (sur•vayz)—views of broad areas, fields, or subjects

grid—a pattern of vertical and horizontal lines that forms squares

and why they built these structures. Paintings on the walls tell some of the story. Objects found inside the buildings tell even more of the story.

Many times archaeologists must **excavate,** or dig, in order to find the objects they seek. But they can't just dig a hole anywhere. A site must be found. Archaeologists find these sites in several ways. They can walk across a field or desert and look at the ground. When they turn up a lot of broken objects, they think they're onto something! They might walk around and search hills for caves. They study old maps. Sometimes a small hill or mound seems like a place where something might be. Archaeologists can also do **surveys** from above. From the air they can see where old walls and houses might have been. When they think they have a site, they take samples. Holes are dug in several places to see if any objects are found. If not, they choose another place.

In 1973, a team of archaeologists led by Johanson returned to Hadar. They went back to the dry riverbed where the tools had been found. A volcano had left ashes in the riverbed. The archaeologists decided this would be a good place to search for bones. What a thrill it was when Johanson found two humanlike bones!

Excavation

Once a site is located, a site map needs to be drawn. Everything that's found must be placed on the map. Before the excavation or dig can begin, a **grid,** or series of squares marked with string, must be made. A datum point, a point from which the lines in a grid are drawn, is set. Everything is marked from that point. To make the grid, rope or string is placed on the ground to form squares. Each square has a number. The numbers are plotted on a grid that looks like a piece of graph paper. Everything that is located is numbered on the grid according to where it was found. No dig is any good unless archaeologists know exactly where every object was found.

As the archaeological team lays out the grid, they decide what kind of information they want to record. They make a form (or chart) on which to take notes. When the grid is in place and all is ready, the dig begins.

Artifacts are recorded on a grid.

One type of dig is called a **vertical** dig. A vertical dig goes in a narrow chute, or tunnel, down into the earth. Then archaeologists examine each layer of earth, or stratum. As the hole is dug, they look at the color and texture of the dirt and what is in it. They look for clues in each layer. If one object is below another object, then the lower object should be older. Sometimes objects have moved from their original layer. This can be due to floods, a volcano, a house being built, or other reasons. When archaeologists see this, they search for other clues.

At Hadar, the researchers used another type of excavation. They dug in a **horizontal** direction. The excavation took place completely on one level and over a larger area. In a horizontal dig, archaeologists look for houses, fireplaces, walls of buildings, remains of animals, bones, food, and large buildings. By figuring out how big the area was, these detectives can guess how many people might have lived there. Once they have excavated one area, they go down another layer. Then they do another horizontal dig.

Collecting Secrets From the Past

Digs don't begin with bulldozers, but with shovels. As soon as objects are found, shovels are replaced with **trowels** and brushes. Archaeologists' tools are brushes, dental probes, tape measures, and tiny toothbrushes. Every piece of dirt is saved and sifted. All the dirt from one small part of the grid is put in a bag. The bag is tagged and numbered. The detectives want to know exactly where things were found. To tell the story, they need to know where in time and space an object was discovered.

When a bag is filled, it is put in a sifter, and water is run over it. Anything that is found is labeled as to where it

Strategy

Interact With Text by identifying the main idea and supporting details.

My Thinking
Main Idea of Excavation: Archaeologists dig to find objects from the past.

Supporting Details:
• They make a grid to keep track of where they find objects.
• A vertical dig is a narrow tunnel into the earth.
• A horizontal dig goes across a large flat area.

Vo•cab•u•lar•y

vertical (**vur**•ti•kuhl)— straight up and down

horizontal (hor•i•**zon**•tl)— level or straight across

trowels (**trow**•uhlz)— small, handheld scoops

was found. Someone takes pictures, someone draws, and another person writes. Teamwork is essential.

Johanson's team carefully brushed and sifted dirt away from the old riverbed in Hadar. In 1974, after months of work, more pieces of bone were found. A part of a skull was found. In all, 40 percent, or almost half, of a humanlike creature was found. Each piece was carefully excavated and recorded. When the pieces were all put together, they had a skeleton. The team called the skeleton Lucy. The name came from "Lucy in the Sky with Diamonds," a popular song at the time. The team sang that song as they worked at the site.

An archaeologist sifts for clues.

Analyzing the Data

Once objects are found and recorded, they are sent to a laboratory. Here the process of finding out the age of the object begins. Until 1950, dating was done by good guesswork and by looking at layers of dirt. Today there are laboratory tests. Archaeologists rely on relative and absolute dating.

Dr. Johanson with Lucy bones

Relative dating means that the scientists think that things found in the same layer are the same age. They connect an object that does not have a date to one that does. Other methods can give an absolute date—a date that is **accurate** within two hundred years. Scientists can find this absolute date by looking at written historical records. They also use radiocarbon dating and Potassium Argon dating. In radiocarbon and Potassium Argon dating, scientists use what they know about how certain substances change over time to determine an object's age.

Strategy

Interact With Text by identifying the main idea and supporting details.

My Thinking
Main Idea of Analyzing the Data: Archaeologists use different methods to date objects they find.

Supporting Details:
• relative dating
• absolute dating
• radiocarbon dating
• Potassium Argon dating

An archaeologist examining skulls in his laboratory

In Africa, the skull of Lucy was dated by Potassium Argon dating. Potassium Argon dating is used on **volcanic ash**. Lucy was found in a bed of volcanic ash. According to this method, Lucy is 3.2 million years old. Johanson's team found 13 more skeletons on the same site. Then they studied all the bones that were found in the area and dated to the same period. They figured out that a band of humanlike creatures had lived there more than 3 million years ago.

Vo•cab•u•lar•y

accurate (ak•yuhr•it)— exact; true

volcanic ash (vol•kan•ik ash) —material released when a volcano erupts

Telling the Story

Just finding objects or looking at ancient buildings doesn't solve any problems. Archaeologists must go back to their hypothesis. Did what they find confirm their guess? Are there more questions? In the case of Lucy, they compared her bones with other bones found at the same site. They also studied what other scientists had written. Then they drew their own conclusions. Yes, she was old. Yes, there were humanlike creatures on the earth millions of years ago. Lucy could stand up, and she could walk on just two feet. But was she an **ancestor** of humans?

Archaeologists don't stop their work when all the clues have been sorted. Instead, they explain the puzzle to others. The work isn't done until they write down all that they have learned. Most of these detectives write about their hypothesis. They tell how they went about proving it—or not proving it—and what they found when they excavated the site. They also tell how they were able to date the objects. Finally, they draw conclusions from their work. Archaeologists' careful search for clues really does make them "history's detectives."

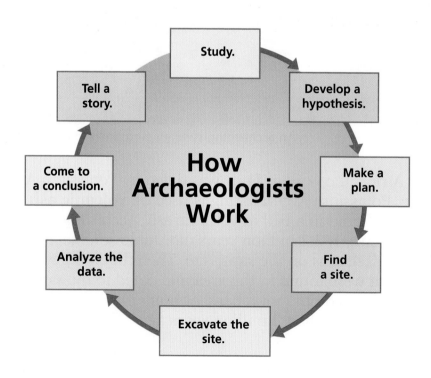

How Archaeologists Work

Study. → Develop a hypothesis. → Make a plan. → Find a site. → Excavate the site. → Analyze the data. → Come to a conclusion. → Tell a story.

Vo·cab·u·lar·y

ancestor (an•ses•tuhr)— a person from whom one is descended

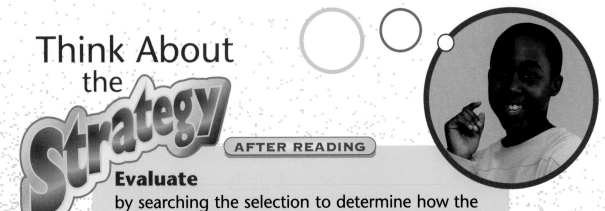

Think About the Strategy

AFTER READING

Evaluate

by searching the selection to determine how the author used evidence to reach conclusions.

My Thinking

This strategy says to evaluate by searching the selection to determine how the author used evidence to reach conclusions, or to reach decisions. The author of this selection used a lot of evidence to write this story.

The author reached the conclusion that all good scientists find answers to questions. Then she told us how archaeologists work through their questions by making plans, searching for data, and going on excavations in order to reach conclusions. The author also reached the conclusion that scientists and archaeologists use special methods to find out the age of objects. Then she told us the different methods of dating that they use.

It seems like the author did a lot of research to find evidence to back up her conclusions.

Graphic organizers help us organize information we read. I think this article can be organized by using a web. I put the main idea or topic of the article in the middle circle. Then I put details about the article at the end of each arm.

Web

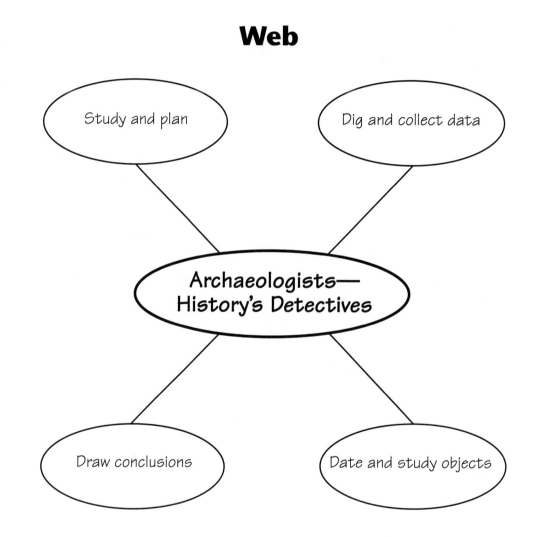

I used my graphic organizer to write a summary of the article. Can you find the information in my summary that came from my web?

A Summary of
Archaeologists—History's Detectives

Archaeologists don't just go around digging things up. Like other scientists, they have a lot of work to do. They study and plan, dig and collect data, date and study objects, and draw conclusions about their work.

Archaeologists start with a problem or idea. They come up with a hypothesis. Then they go about trying to prove their hypothesis. Archaeologists spend a lot of time studying. They do surveys and study old maps to find good places to dig.

Archaeologists go many places to dig. They look in riverbeds, in swamps, in the desert, in the jungle, and in ice. They also dig on mountains and under the ocean. They are in search of data to collect. They look for artifacts, ecofacts, and features. Then they use a grid to divide the site into small areas. That way, they can record where they found a bit of pottery, an old tool, or a piece of bone. Archaeologists dig very carefully, using tiny shovels. Then they use toothbrushes to brush away dirt.

Archaeologists study whatever they find. They figure out how old objects are and they date them. They use different methods to date objects. They also study when and how the objects were used. It is much like working on a big scientific puzzle.

Archaeologists must complete one more step. They draw conclusions. They decide whether their findings prove that their hypothesis is correct. Many times, what they dug up makes them ask even more questions!

There is much to learn about archaeology. And archaeologists have a lot to study and examine. They must develop a hypothesis and determine where to dig. Much work is put into examining and proving the hypothesis. Archaeologists work hard, but they must love their work!

Introduction
My introductory paragraph tells readers what they are about to read.

Body
Each paragraph has information from one arm of my web. The first body paragraph tells readers about how archaeologists study and plan. The next paragraph tells how they dig and collect data. Then, my next paragraph tells about dating and studying the objects they find. The last body paragraph tells readers that archaeologists must draw conclusions.

Conclusion
I concluded my paper by summarizing my main ideas.

Word Parts

Detectives look for clues—or **sleuth**—whenever they're on a case. Like a detective, you can use word clues to figure out word meanings. Try the good detective approach of dividing the word into smaller parts. Each part has a meaning.

Start by dividing a word that you know well such as *basketball*. The word part *ball* indicates a sport or a game. The word part *basket* relates to how the game is played. You will often find a word's meaning by first finding the meaning of its parts.

Look at the word *Acropolis* from "Archaeologists—History's Detectives." *Acropolis* is a word with two parts:

- *Acros* is from the Greek *akros*. It means "the highest or height."
- *Polis* is Greek. It means "city."

When you put the two word parts together, what do you get? You get the word *Acropolis*, the word for "highest city."

> Use your word part detective skills, as well as information from the example above, to answer the following questions.
>
> **1.** If the word part *phobia* means "fear," what does *acrophobia* mean?
>
> **2.** What is another word for a trapeze artist? (Hint: It ends with *bat*.)
>
> **3.** What is the capital city of Indiana?
>
> Let's do some more detective work. Look at the following words or word parts and their meanings. Join them with the word part *-ologist,* which means "one who studies," to create new words. Write the new words on a separate sheet of paper. Then, write their definitions and a sentence for each new word.
>
> **1.** *meteor,* which means "matter from outside Earth's atmosphere"
>
> **2.** *geo,* which means "Earth"

Readers' Theater

Read the following script with a partner. Marco and Julie are friends and coworkers. They have been working together at an archaeological site for a long time. Make sure your voices express the friendship and fun they are having.

Fluency
TIP

Be sure to express surprise in your voices when the characters make an interesting discovery.

Julie and Marco Meet Darcy
At a site in Hadar in 1974

Marco (singing): "Darcy sails the seven seas, but when will she return home?"

Julie: In just one more hour we will be able to leave the site and go eat.

Marco: I can't wait to eat! (continues singing) "Darcy sails the seven seas—"

Julie (interrupts): I can't wait for you to stop singing.

Marco: I wonder what's for lunch.

Julie: You never met a meal you didn't like.

Marco: In this heat, it's the juice and water I need more than the—

Julie (interrupts): Hey, I think I hit something.

Marco: Where?

Julie: Over here! I'm digging at number D2 on the grid.

Marco: It's probably just another big rock in the middle of all this volcanic ash. You get more excited when your trowel hits a rock than I do when I hear the lunch bell!

Julie: No, really, Marco. Look here, just under my trowel!

Marco: Wow, it just might be more than a rock. It looks like bones, Julie. And I think it's more than one!

Julie: Wait until Dr. Johnson sees these. There might be enough bones here to make a whole skeleton, a whole person from millions of years ago!

Marco: I wonder if you found a male or a female.

Julie: Yeah, I wonder what her name was? What do you think we should call her?

Marco: I don't know. Let's tell the others.

Julie: Yes, let's go.

Marco (singing): "Darcy sails the seven seas, but when will she return to me?"

Think About the Strategies

BEFORE READING

Activate Prior Knowledge

by looking at the title, headings, pictures, and graphics to decide what I know about this topic.

 Write notes on your own paper to tell how you used this strategy.

DURING READING

Interact With Text

by identifying the main idea and supporting details.

 When you come to a red button like this ⦿, write notes on your own paper to tell how you used this strategy.

Ancient Timekeepers

If a friend asked you how many days it was until summer, what would you do? You would probably look at a calendar and count the number of days between now and then. It's easy to take inventions such as our modern-day calendar for granted. But what did people do before modern calendars? How did they know when it was time for summer to begin? How did they know when to prepare for winter?

Stonehenge: Full of Mystery

Imagine 40 gigantic stones, many as tall as 25 feet, rising from a hilltop. This is Stonehenge. Stonehenge was built long, long ago. There were 3 main periods of building, beginning around 3,000 B.C. That makes the **monument**

Vo•**cab**•u•lar•y

monument
(**mon**•yuh•muhnt)—
a structure put up to remember someone or something or to mark a place or position

[**67**]

about 5,000 years old. It was finished 1,400 years later, in about 1,600 B.C.

It is believed that many generations of people helped build Stonehenge. They built it on the Salisbury [**sawlz**•ber•ee] Plain in southern England. Stonehenge was obviously very important. But what exactly is it?

We could look for clues in its name. *Henge* is an old English word. It means "to hang." Some say the structure got this name because the stones looked like they were hanging in midair. Others say it's because criminals were hanged from Stonehenge's crosspieces. *Crosspieces* are the long stones that lie across the top of the ancient structure. No one is really certain how Stonehenge got its name.

Bull's-Eye

If you walk up to Stonehenge, it looks like a scattered mess of **immense** stones. They seem to be standing in a circle. Still, you can't quite make out any pattern. But if you were to look at Stonehenge from above, you would see an amazing design. The outer stones form two large circles, one inside the other. Inside the center ring is another set of large stones that form a horseshoe. Surrounding all

Using Text Features

Map Review the sketch of Stonehenge. Then work with a partner. Take turns describing the design of Stonehenge. Make sure to point out the Altar Stone inside the horseshoe ring, and the straight line that goes from the Altar Stone to the Heel Stone.

Vo•**cab**•u•lar•y

immense (i•**mens**)— extremely large

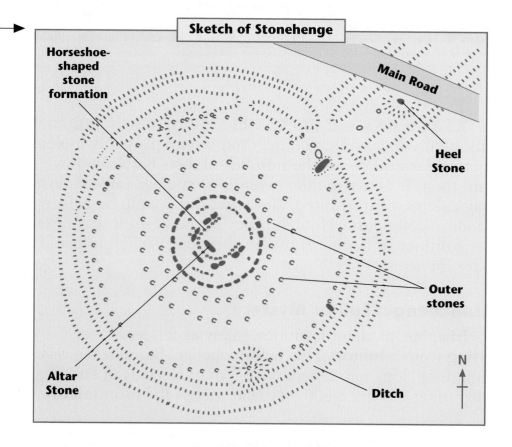

Sketch of Stonehenge

Horseshoe-shaped stone formation

Main Road

Heel Stone

Outer stones

Altar Stone

Ditch

N

these massive stones is a large ditch. This ditch forms another circle. In the center of the rings is a tall stone called the Altar Stone. From above, Stonehenge looks like a target with a bull's-eye in the center.

Outside all the rings is one of the biggest stones of all. It is called the Heel Stone. At 16 feet high and about 35 tons, it's almost as heavy as an 18-wheeled truck! Like a slumping giant, the Heel Stone leans toward the main circle of stones.

The huge stones look strange, magical, and even a little scary. There are many legends about the **origin** of these stones. Some people believe they are "dancing giants" that turned to stone. Others believe the magician Merlin made the massive stones fly to England from Ireland. Still others say the stones were brought to the site by an evil spirit. This last legend also explains how the Heel Stone got its name. The story goes that when the evil spirit built Stonehenge, a **monk** kicked one of the stones with his heel. His heel was so strong, he almost tipped over the massive rock that is now called the Heel Stone.

Nobody knows for sure *how* the ring of stones came to be. But some believe they know part of the reason *why* Stonehenge exists.

Strategy

Interact With Text by identifying the main idea and supporting details.

Write notes on your own paper to tell how you used this strategy.

Megaliths and Barrows

The massive stones at Stonehenge are called megaliths. This word is from two Greek words—*mega*, meaning "large" and *lithos*, meaning "stone." One of the circles is formed from smaller stones called bluestones. Although smaller than the megaliths, some bluestones weigh up to 5 tons. These unique stones came from only one place in the world—a mountain range in Wales. Archaeologists believe the bluestones were brought from these mountains— 130 miles away—to Stonehenge! Why would people put so much effort into Stonehenge? We can

Close-up view of Stonehenge

Vo·cab·u·lar·y

origin (**or**•uh•jin)—source; beginning

monk (mungk)—a man who is a member of a religious order and lives according to its rules

only guess that if ancient people built something so monstrous, it was for a very important reason.

Archaeologists have found **barrows** around the Stonehenge area. Barrows are mounds of dirt that cover burial sites. That leads some people to believe that Stonehenge was used as a burial site. Most archaeologists agree that Stonehenge was built as a place to perform ceremonies. But it is believed that there was yet another use for this monument. There is evidence that Stonehenge was a giant calendar!

An Amazing Shadow

The people who labored for years to build Stonehenge were farmers. This community needed to know when to plant crops and when to **harvest** them. If they misjudged when to begin those tasks, they could ruin their crops. If they weren't "on time," they would starve.

Stonehenge helped the farmers keep track of important days. The **summer solstice** is the longest day of the year. We now know that it usually falls on June 21st or 22nd. But the farmers didn't have a calendar like we do. So they used the sun and Stonehenge to help them know exactly when the solstice arrived.

On the morning of the solstice, the sun rose directly behind the Heel Stone. The stone's shadow fell exactly between two stones standing at the entrance to the monument. At first light, the Heel Stone's shadow touched the Altar Stone at the very center of the circle. On the day that this occurred, the message to the people of Stonehenge was clear: Spring was over, and summer had arrived!

Vo•cab•u•lar•y

barrows (**bar**•ohz)—large mounds of earth or stones placed over a burial site

harvest (**har**•vist)— to gather crops

summer solstice (**sol**•stis)— the day on which summer begins; the longest day of the year

Stonehenge at sunrise

Telling Time by the Sun

We have an idea about *why* Stonehenge was built, but *how* was it built? After all, there's nothing easy about moving huge, heavy rocks. And moving them hundreds of miles makes the task even harder to imagine. Once the stones were brought to the site, how did the builders know where to put them?

We don't know the answer for sure, but we can make a good guess. Ancient people had no computers. They also had no clocks. There was only one way they could judge time. They had to watch the sun, the moon, and the stars.

Stonehenge's builders probably tracked the sun's path over and over during the 1,200 years the monument was being built. They watched how the angle of shadows changed from day to day. The workers marked the ground to **plot** those changes. When they were sure where the Heel Stone's shadow would fall on summer solstice morning, they finally moved the Heel Stone into place. From then on, that shadow would welcome the arrival of summer. Or so they thought.

As it turns out, the Heel Stone no longer marks the summer solstice correctly. The stone hasn't moved—Earth has. Our planet's tilt has shifted a little since the stone was first placed. This fact was discovered in 1905 by Sir Norman Lockyer, a British **astronomer**. Knowing about Earth's tilt helped Lockyer to **calculate** the date of Stonehenge's completion—about 3,600 years ago.

Were There Other Timekeepers?

The mystery surrounding Stonehenge is just one of many in the world. Its history was hard to piece together because so few clues exist. The Maya, however, have left behind written records. These records have helped archaeologists learn amazing things about these ancient peoples of Mexico.

Mayan Calendars

The Maya lived in Mexico for about 800 years—until around A.D. 900.

They believed that time moved in **cycles**. Each cycle lasted 5,125 years. The belief was that at the end of a cycle, the sun and world are destroyed. Then everything is

Strategy

Interact With Text by identifying the main idea and supporting details.

Write notes on your own paper to tell how you used this strategy.

Vo·cab·u·lar·y

plot—to mark

astronomer (uh•**stron**•uh•muhr)— a scientist who studies the stars and planets

calculate (**kal**•kyuh•layt)— to figure out by using math

cycles (**sy**•kuhlz)—patterns that repeat over and over

A Mayan temple

reborn and the cycle starts over. The latest cycle began on August 12, 3113 B.C.

Mayan timekeepers used a calendar called the Long Count to keep track of long cycles of time. The smallest unit of time in the Long Count was called the kin. One kin was equal to our day. Twenty kins made up one uinal. One uinal was equal to what we would call a 20-day month. Finally, 18 uinals made up 1 tun—the Mayan term for 1 year.

The Maya also added 5 extra days to their year. Those 5 days were considered unlucky. The 360 kins plus 5 unlucky kins made a 365-day year. Today we know that 1 year is 365 and one-quarter days long. So the Mayan calendar was off a bit—but not by much. We don't know how they corrected it.

Another Mayan calendar was used along with the Long Count. It was called the Calendar Round. It followed a 260-day year. This calendar was made up of 2 elements—

the Sacred Almanac and the Vague Year. Archaeologists believe that the Calendar Round was used to mark religious ceremonies.

The Sacred Almanac was part of the heritage that all civilized Mexican nations shared. This element of the Calendar Round was represented by 2 wheels. They fit together like gears. One wheel had 13 slots which were numbered from 1 to 13. The other wheel had 20 "teeth," and each tooth had its own name. Each day, the wheels rotated together. That day would be given a name that combined the name of the tooth and the number of the slot. So, instead of naming a day July 5th, for example, the Calendar Round might name the day Three Lizard. "Three" came from the slot number on the first wheel. "Lizard" came from the tooth name on the second wheel. When "slot three" and "tooth lizard" came together, the day was called "Three Lizard."

The 365-day Vague Year was the second element of the Calendar Round. It was made up of 18 twenty-day months. Five extra days were added to the end of the Vague Year. By **modifying** the Vague Year and the Sacred Almanac, the Calendar Round was created with a total of 18,980 days! This calendar started over every 52 solar years.

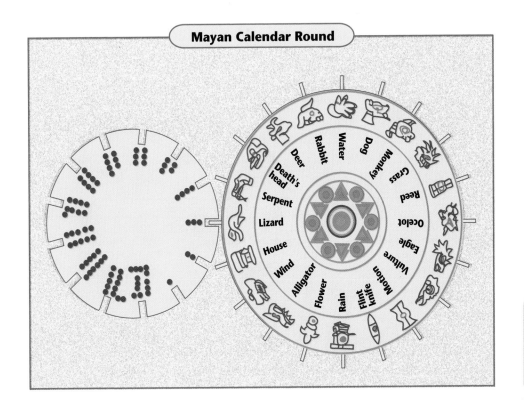

Mayan Calendar Round

Strategy

Interact With Text by identifying the main idea and supporting details.

Write notes on your own paper to tell how you used this strategy.

Vo•cab•u•lar•y

modifying (mod•uh•fy•ing)— changing slightly

Predicting Solar Eclipses

These fascinating Mayan people had another interesting ability. They seemed to be able to predict solar eclipses. Solar eclipses occur when the moon moves directly in between the sun and Earth. The sun seems to disappear. Everything becomes dark and still for a few minutes. Much Mayan writing was **devoted** to solar eclipses. It seems that they were very important to the Maya. These ancient people even predicted eclipses that would have appeared somewhere else on Earth. That's quite amazing because they could not have seen those eclipses from Mexico!

The Maya built their own version of a solar clock. Around A.D. 300, they built a large **pyramid** at a place called Uaxactún, on the Yucatán Peninsula. East of this pyramid—toward the rising sun—the Maya built three small temples in a line running north to south. Mayan priests stood on the large pyramid to watch the sun rise. If the sun rose directly over the northern temple, they knew it was the summer solstice, the longest day of the year. At the winter solstice—the shortest day of the year—the sun rose over the southern temple. And at the two days each year called **equinoxes**—when day and night are the same length—the sun rose over the center temple.

So, just as the farmers used the sun and Stonehenge to track the time of year, the Maya used the sun and a pyramid.

Vo•**cab**•u•lar•y

devoted (di•**voh**•tid)—giving time or attention entirely to; having or showing loyalty

pyramid (**pir**•uh•mid)— a large structure having four triangular walls that meet in a point at the top

eqinoxes (ee•kwuh•noks•es) —the two times of the year when day and night are equal in length everywhere on Earth

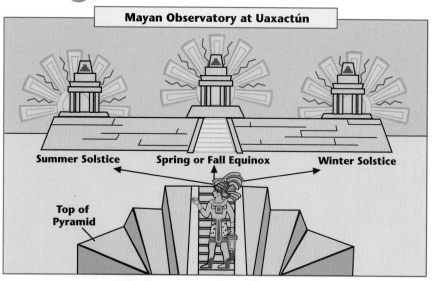

Mayan Observatory at Uaxactún

Summer Solstice   Spring or Fall Equinox   Winter Solstice

Top of Pyramid

This diagram shows how the Mayan people used their own solar calendar to plot the seasons.

Timekeepers

The tracking of time has come a long way. Before the development of the written calendar, people used the sun, stars, and moon to tell time. Today we know that these earliest timekeepers were not exact measurements. Yet, it's hard not to admire the ways ancient people made "sense" of the passing of time. To this day, we marvel at the beautiful structures these ancient people contributed to history.

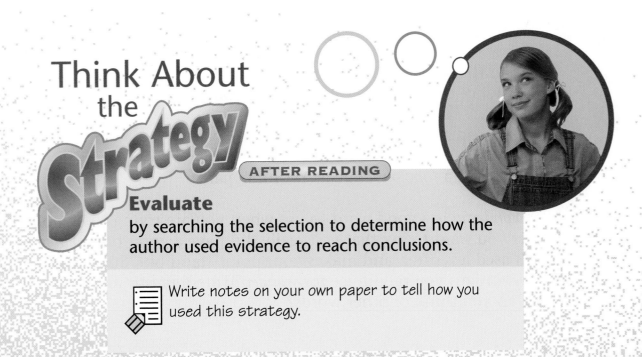

Think About the Strategy

AFTER READING

Evaluate

by searching the selection to determine how the author used evidence to reach conclusions.

Write notes on your own paper to tell how you used this strategy.

Synonyms

You may have heard the saying "When it rains, it pours." *Rains* and *pours* are **synonyms**. Synonyms are words that have the same or almost the same meaning. When a friend asks if you had a good time at a birthday party, you might say, "I had a *great* time!" or "I had a *fantastic* time." *Great* and *fantastic* are synonyms.

Writers use synonyms when they want to write about similar ideas, but they don't want to keep repeating the same words. Finding synonyms for overused words can make your own writing more exciting, too. You can find synonyms in a thesaurus.

Read the following sentences. How does the meaning of the sentence change depending on the word used?

I had a *wonderful* time at Yvonne's party.

I had a *fabulous* time at Yvonne's party.

Wonderful is a good word to use when you are trying to be polite, or you want to say that you really did have a good time. *Fabulous* is used less often and makes your point stand out. Some other synonyms you might use for *wonderful* are *fantastic* and *terrific*. Can you think of other words?

In the selection "Ancient Timekeepers," you read at least six synonyms for the word *big*. Reread the section. Can you find six?

Poetry

Reading poems requires a good sense of rhythm.
Practice reading this poem out loud until you can read
it smoothly and with a good rhythm.

Be sure to make your voice sound like it is asking questions in the first stanza of the poem.

Three Watches

Did Merlin fly his massive stones
From Ireland to English soil?
Or were bluestones carried the miles
From Wales by many men's toil?

Yes, someone placed these megaliths,
Like a poem with all its rhymes,
In patterns so that farmers
Had a chance to tell the time.

In Mexico the Maya built
Pyramids to track the seasons.
They predicted solar eclipses
When darkness reigns for good reason.

My own small watch can tell the time
For lunchtime without a guess,
Though not as mighty as Stonehenge
My small watch weighs a lot less!

Think About
the
Strategies

BEFORE READING

Activate Prior Knowledge

by looking at the title, headings, pictures, and graphics to decide what I know about this topic.

DURING READING

Interact With Text

by identifying the main idea and supporting details.

AFTER READING

Evaluate

by searching the selection to determine how the author used evidence to reach conclusions.

 Use your own paper to jot notes to apply these Before, During, and After Reading Strategies. In this selection, you will choose when to stop, think, and respond.

Cracking the Code of Hammurabi

What do you think of a law that says that if a son strikes his father, his hand may be cut off? What about a law that says that if one person hurts another in a fight, the one who caused the injury pays for the medical treatment?

The first law sounds severe and cruel. The second law sounds fair. Believe it or not, both of these laws were in effect in 1750 B.C. They are part of what we now call the Code of Hammurabi [ham•uh•**rah**•bee]. Although we know a lot about this ancient code now, that wasn't always the case.

Discovery in the Desert

In December 1901, French archaeologist Jean-Vincent Scheil and his team were digging at a site called Susa. Susa is located in the Middle East, on land that is now part of Iran.

At the top of the stone found at Susa, Hammurabi is shown receiving laws from the Babylonian sun god.

The digging had been hard, slow, and sometimes dangerous. The site was in the middle of a very hot desert. Windblown sand burned the men's eyes and filled their noses. Biting sand flies filled the air. Poisonous snakes, scorpions, and spiders **lurked** on the ground!

But the long, difficult hours paid off when the team uncovered a huge black stone! It stood nearly eight feet tall and was shaped like a pointed index finger.

The top of the large stone showed an image of a king. Thousands of words, carved in an ancient language, covered the stone. The king pictured on the stone is Hammurabi, one of the ancient world's strongest leaders. Hammurabi had many successes, but he is best known for writing a set of laws.

The "Fertile Crescent"

The black stone that Scheil discovered didn't belong in Susa. It had been stolen and taken there around 1200 B.C. The stone had been carved hundreds of years earlier in the powerful kingdom of Babylonia. Located to the west of Susa, Babylonia was on land that is now part of Iraq. That part of the world was called Mesopotamia, or "Land Between the Rivers." This land was between the Tigris and Euphrates rivers.

For thousands of years, long before Babylonia, the area's rich farmland and fertile crops supported many cities and civilizations. Because of this, Mesopotamia was known as the "Fertile Crescent."

One of the first civilizations in the Fertile Crescent was called Sumer. The Sumerians gave us many important inventions, including the wheel. The Sumerians first used the wheel around 6500 B.C., about 8,500 years ago. They used the wheel and cattle for plowing to plant crops.

Sumerian bronze statue of a harnessed chariot

The Sumerians invented something else that you use every day. In fact, you're using it right now: written **symbols** that express ideas—words!

Carvings in Soft Clay

Writing was invented because people who traded things needed a way to keep track of what they bought and sold. The Sumerians began carving symbols into flat slabs of soft clay. Today, we call their writing *cuneiform*. The word means "wedge-shaped." People used a pointed, wedge-shaped tool to carve into the clay.

The Sumerians used clay because paper hadn't been invented. The clay slabs were called tablets. The cuneiform was carved into a tablet and then left in the sun to dry. The clay hardened as it dried. As a result, many of the tablets have lasted to this day.

Among those tablets is the oldest written story in the world. It is called the Legend of Gilgamesh. It includes a tale of a great flood, in which people survived by building a boat. The story is similar to the story of Noah's Ark.

A clay cuneiform tablet from Mesopotamia

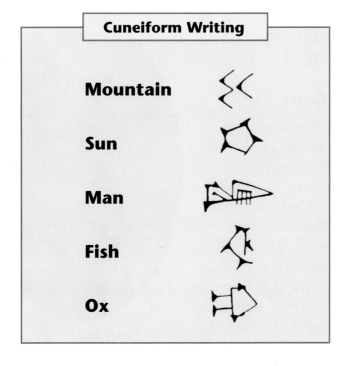

Cuneiform Writing

Mountain	
Sun	
Man	
Fish	
Ox	

Vo•cab•u•lar•y

symbols (**sim**•buhlz)—things that stand for something else

From Pictures to Letters

In early cuneiform writing, people used pictures for whole words. Such pictures are called **ideograms**. The well-known symbols on Egyptian monuments, called **hieroglyphics**—pictures or symbols that represented words or sounds in the writing system used in ancient Egypt—are ideograms.

Over time, however, the cuneiform changed. The pictures changed into **abstract** symbols, a kind of early shorthand. As more time passed, people began assigning these symbols to individual sounds. They created an alphabet, similar to the English you're reading here. Some of the letters of cuneiform even look like letters used in English and other languages!

The Great Mystery

In 1901, when Jean-Vincent Scheil and his team dug up the large black stone at Susa, many **scholars** could read and understand its cuneiform writing. But if the stone had been found only 50 years earlier, no one would have been able to read it. No one would have been able to translate or interpret the meaning of the information that the stone contained.

Usually, the work of translation is slow and hard. It is just like digging, only cleaner. Also, you don't run into snakes and spiders! But one man did risk his life while trying to solve the great mystery of cuneiform.

The Place of the Gods

Henry Rawlinson was a young officer in the British army. He loved ancient history and languages. In 1835, Rawlinson was sent to a post in northwestern Iran. There he visited a huge carving at the Rock of Behistun [bay•his•toon]. The local people called it the Place of the Gods.

The Rock of Behistun is a huge, flat stone cliff. A giant figure of a king is carved on its face, about 300 feet up.

Sir Henry Rawlinson

He has a bow in his hand, and he stands on the neck of another man—possibly a beaten enemy.

Rawlinson was most interested in what was beneath the carving. It was a large written message, about 60 feet wide and 22 feet high. Because no one could read the message, no one could name the king in the carving.

Scaling the Heights

For the next 12 years, Henry Rawlinson copied all the writings on the rock. But he didn't do it from the ground. Instead, time after time, he climbed up the steep cliff. It was hard and risky because the cliff wall rose straight up. The slightest mistake would have sent Rawlinson to his death!

Rawlinson's dangerous work paid off. He discovered that the message on the rock was written in three different languages. It was like the signs you see in airports that give the same information in English, Spanish, and Japanese.

Cuneiform was one of the languages carved at Behistun. The other two were types of Persian, the language of Iran. One of them was Old Persian, and Rawlinson understood it. He used his knowledge of Old Persian to translate the message in cuneiform.

Over the next 10 years, Rawlinson and many other scholars solved the mystery of cuneiform writing. They translated thousands of cuneiform tablets. Those tablets told about Mesopotamia, Sumer, Babylonia, and a king named Hammurabi.

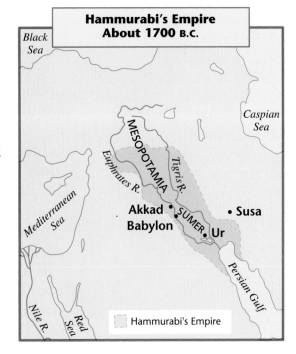

The Words—and Laws—of a King

When Hammurabi became king of Babylonia around 1792 B.C., his armies began conquering Sumer and the rest of Mesopotamia. Hammurabi also began building a strong civilization. He understood that in order to do that, people needed laws. The words on the black stone are a system of laws that we have named the Code of Hammurabi.

The Beginnings of Law

Hammurabi's ideas were strong and simple. They are similar to the ideas behind the U.S. Constitution. For one thing,

A picture of daily life in Babylonia

the laws meant that people could not be subject to the **whim** of a ruler. If someone had a **grievance** or committed a crime, the code of laws told what would happen to him or her.

Like our modern law, Hammurabi's code grouped laws by topic. The code separated laws relating to crimes from laws relating to contracts. It allowed judges, not the king, to decide cases. It also allowed witnesses to testify, either for or against the person making a claim. In some cases, juries could be formed.

A Law for Everything

Hammurabi's code covered all kinds of issues. Some of his laws set down punishments for crimes, such as theft and assault. Some laws defined the duties of people who acted as mayors and police officers. Some laws told how people could borrow and lend money, and how they could rent property.

Laws placed limits on how much money people could charge for services. The limits covered people such as doctors, boatmen, farmers, and builders. There was a long list of laws about marriage and family issues. The list went on and on. In all, there were 282 laws.

The idea that made the code famous was the one that established Hammurabi's system of justice. The code read: "If a man has put out the eye of a man . . . they shall put out his eye. If he has broken a bone . . . they shall break his bone."

Today, Hammurabi's code is known by the phrase "An eye for an eye, and a tooth for a tooth."

Vo·**cab**·u·lar·y

whim (wim)—a sudden wish or desire

grievance (gree•vuhns)— a complaint

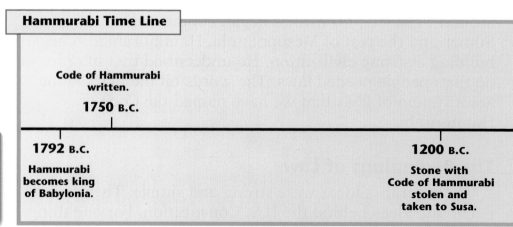

Hammurabi Time Line

Code of Hammurabi written.
1750 B.C.

1792 B.C.
Hammurabi becomes king of Babylonia.

1200 B.C.
Stone with Code of Hammurabi stolen and taken to Susa.

A Harsh Set of Laws

The idea of taking someone's eye is very harsh by today's standards. What's more, Hammurabi's code punished many crimes even more severely—by death. A person could be put to death for stealing. A person could even be killed for performing magic tricks without the king's permission.

Hammurabi's code also set up three classes of society in Babylonia: **aristocrats,** poor people, and slaves. Aristocrats often had lighter punishments than poor people and slaves.

Not a Perfect System, but a Start

As far as we know, this code was fairer than anything that had been used earlier. Before the code, most rulers would kill or punish anyone for any reason. Hammurabi began to change all that. He allowed people to pay fines—amounts of money—to escape some punishments. For example, people could pay fines to escape being put to death.

Hammurabi's code was not the first body of laws. People thought that it was because it was discovered first. Scholars have learned that Hammurabi borrowed many of his laws and rulings from earlier codes.

Even so, Hammurabi's code began many of the important **traditions** that are the basis for our modern legal system. It's amazing to think that these traditions have their roots in a black stone slab nearly 4,000 years old!

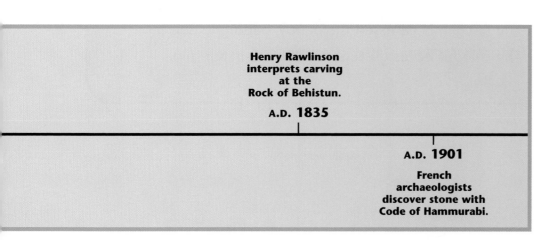

Henry Rawlinson interprets carving at the Rock of Behistun.

A.D. **1835**

A.D. **1901**

French archaeologists discover stone with Code of Hammurabi.

Vo•cab•u•lar•y

aristocrats (uh•**ris**•tuh•krats) —people who belong to a social class, based on birth, whose members often enjoy more wealth and status than the rest of society

traditions (truh•**dish**•uhnz)—customs that pass from generation to generation

The Context Clue Code

When you read unfamiliar words, it can stop you in your tracks. Often, however, there are clues in the same sentence that give you enough meaning so that you can keep on reading. These clues are called **context clues**. Using context clues is a little like "cracking a code." Once you've cracked the code, you can keep on reading.

Look at an example in the selection "Cracking the Code of Hammurabi."

*Poisonous snakes, scorpions, and spiders **lurked** on the ground!*

This sentence tells you that these three animals are all doing the same thing on the ground. What else do you know about snakes, spiders, and scorpions that can tell you what *lurked* means? These creatures usually lie in wait, ready to strike their next prey. So, *lurked* must mean "sat and waited or sneaked up on something."

Read the following sentences. Then on a separate sheet of paper write the meanings of the words in boldface. Briefly explain what clues helped you find the meaning of each word.

1. When we turned on the light, the **fleeing** mouse was so quick, we saw only its tail.

2. At the crowded park, pigeons **hovered** above family picnics, waiting for crumbs.

3. Busy flies **whirled** around the discarded apple core.

4. The girl gently **caressed** the puppy, petting its soft fur.

5. The colorful leaves **glistened** in the bright sunshine.

Historical Document

Practice reading the Preamble to the U.S. Constitution in a loud and strong voice. Pretend that you are reading this for the first time to your friends and neighbors. Read it so that those who hear you will know it is important.

Fluency TIP

Be sure to pause slightly at commas so that readers will have a chance to take in the ideas in the Preamble.

The United States and Its "Code"

One of the most important documents in the United States is the Constitution. The Preamble to the Constitution does not actually establish law, but it describes the source of law, which is "the people." The Preamble also describes the kind of law that the people who wrote the Constitution hoped to create. In some ways, the Preamble is more important than individual laws, because it is a clue to the shape that all laws in the United States were supposed to take.

The Preamble and Constitution were adopted by a convention of the states on September 17, 1787, and were later ratified by the states of the new United States of America.

Preamble to U.S. Constitution

We the People of the United States, in Order to form a more perfect Union, establish Justice, insure domestic Tranquility, provide for the common defense, promote the general Welfare, and secure the Blessings of Liberty to ourselves and our Posterity, do ordain and establish this Constitution for the United States of America.

Steps in a Process

Layers in a Vertical Archaeological Dig

This diagram shows the artifacts exposed in a dig in the United States. Study the diagram and answer the questions on the next page.

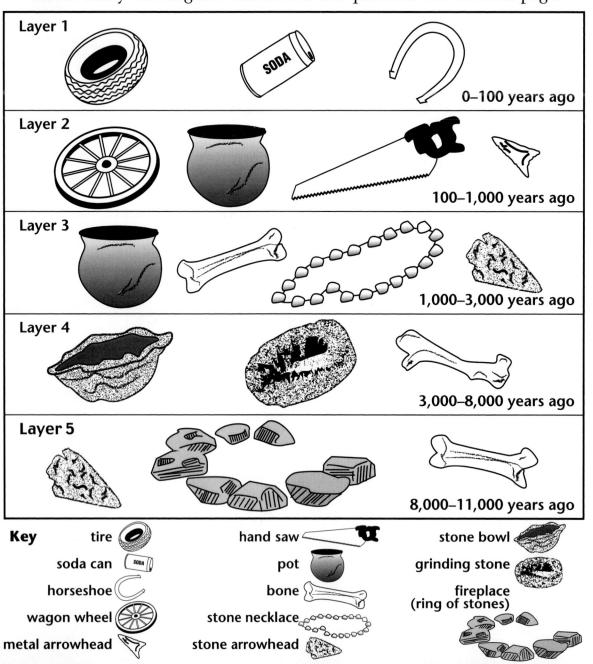

Layer 1 — 0–100 years ago

Layer 2 — 100–1,000 years ago

Layer 3 — 1,000–3,000 years ago

Layer 4 — 3,000–8,000 years ago

Layer 5 — 8,000–11,000 years ago

Key
tire
soda can
horseshoe
wagon wheel
metal arrowhead
hand saw
pot
bone
stone necklace
stone arrowhead
stone bowl
grinding stone
fireplace (ring of stones)

Discussion Questions

Answer these questions with a partner or on a separate sheet of paper.

1. Which layer contains the most recent artifacts? Which layer contains the oldest artifacts?

2. Why is the stone bowl buried so deeply?
   a. It is heavy, so it sank deeper into the soil.
   b. It was used by people very long ago.
   c. The people who used it buried it very deeply.
   d. People no longer carve bowls out of stone.

3. In which layer would objects from your life be buried?

4. When did the people living in this area first start to make and use pottery?
   a. 0–100 years ago
   b. 100–1,000 years ago
   c. 1,000–3,000 years ago
   d. 3,000–8,000 years ago

5. What did people use to make arrowheads before they used metal? How do you know?

6. The second layer includes no horseshoes, but the wagon wheel suggests that horseshoes probably are nearby. An archaeological dig cannot uncover all the artifacts in an area. Is a dig still a good tool for learning about history? Explain your answer.

7. Which sentence best describes how the archaeology of this area would be affected if the ground were plowed up to plant crops?
   a. It would be easier for scientists to study the artifacts.
   b. The relative ages of the artifacts would be difficult to determine.
   c. More people would see and appreciate the artifacts.
   d. The artifacts would get buried deeper.

8. How would this dig change if it were horizontal instead of vertical?
   a. Only one layer or period would be exposed, uncovering more artifacts from that period.
   b. More layers or periods would be exposed, uncovering more artifacts from all the periods.
   c. The dig would look the same, but it would be a series of holes.
   d. The dig would be deeper, uncovering older artifacts.

EXPLORE MORE

Write a Report
Research and write a report on the work of Donald Johanson, the archaeologist featured in "Archaeologists—History's Detectives." Find out about some of the other digs that he has worked on and what his work has revealed about ancient cultures. Be sure to include photographs or illustrations with your report.

Create a Model
Work in a small group to create a model of Stonehenge or the Mayan Calendar Round. You may want to use modeling clay to represent the stones and use construction paper to make the toothed wheels of the Calendar Round.

Set Up a Museum
Work in a small group to set up a mock museum. Make artifacts out of modeling clay, papier-mâché, construction paper, and other art supplies. Make up a history for the artifacts. Tell about where they were found, what they are, how old they are, and what significance they might have to science today.

Write a Report
Conduct further research on Stonehenge. Write a report about some of the theories that have been developed to explain Stonehenge. Include quotes from experts. Also include charts, graphs, maps, and other visual aids to support your findings.

Chart Artifacts
Work in another small group to chart the artifacts the first group "discovered." Make up a site location and prepare a site map. Create a grid and place all artifacts on the map. Decide what information to record. Make a chart on which to take notes.

Role-Play a Trial
Role-play a trial in the time of Hammurabi. Have your teacher select an appropriate crime of that time period. Assign a judge, jury, the accused, and attorneys. In a follow-up discussion, talk about how our modern legal system compares to Hammurabi's code.

Related Books

Avi-Yonah, Michael. *Dig This! How Archaeologists Uncover Our Past.* Runestone Press, 1993.

Chrisp, Peter. *The Aztecs.* Raintree Steck-Vaughn, 2000.

Crosher, Judith. *Technology in the Time of the Maya.* Raintree Steck-Vaughn, 1998.

Devereux, Paul. *Archaeology: The Study of Our Past.* Gareth Stevens Publishing, 2002.

Green, Meg. *Buttons, Bones, and the Organ-Grinder's Monkey: Tales of Historical Archaeology.* Linnet Books, 2001.

Greenberg, Lorna. *Digging Into the Past: Pioneers of Archaeology.* Franklin Watts, 2001.

Landau, Elaine. *The Babylonians.* The Millbrook Press, 1997.

Maestro, Betsy. *The Story of Clocks and Calendars: Marking a Millennium.* Lothrop, Lee and Shepard, 1999.

McIntosh, Jane. *Archaeology.* Dorling Kindersley, 2000.

Panchyk, Richard. *Archaeology for Kids: Uncovering the Mysteries of Our Past.* Chicago Review Press, 2001.

Williams, Brian. *Calendars.* Smart Apple Media, 2003.

Interesting Web Sites

Archaeology and Archaeologists

http://www.archaeology.org

http://news.nationalgeographic.com/news/archaeology.html

Stonehenge and Mayan Calendars

http://www.webexhibits.com/calendars/calendar-mayan.html

http://www.michielb.nl/maya

http://www.physics.nist.gov/GenInt/Time/time.html

http://www.greatbuildings.com/buildings/stonehenge.html

Hammurabi's Code

http://www.phillipmartin.info/hammurabi/homepage.htm

Web sites have been carefully researched for accuracy, content, and appropriateness. However, teachers and caregivers are reminded that Web sites are subject to change. Internet use should always be monitored.

Unit 3 Strategies

BEFORE READING

Set a Purpose

by using the title and headings to write questions that I can answer while I am reading.

DURING READING

Clarify Understanding

by using photographs, charts, and other graphics to help me understand what I'm reading.

AFTER READING

Respond

by drawing logical conclusions about the topic.

LEARN
the **strategies**
in the selection
Robbers of the Seas
page 95

PRACTICE
the *strategies*
in the selection
Fearsome Females of the Seas
page 109

APPLY
the *strategies*
in the selection
The Reign and Ruin of Piracy
page 121

Think About
the
Strategies

BEFORE READING

Set a Purpose

by using the title and headings to write questions that I can answer while I am reading.

My Thinking

This strategy says to set a purpose for reading by using the title and headings to write questions that I can answer while I'm reading. After the introduction, the first heading is, "The Beginnings." I can ask the question, "What and where were the beginnings of piracy?" Another heading is, "The Pirate's Life." I can ask, "What was the life of a pirate like?" I really want to know what the answer to that question is. Another question I might ask is: "Who were Francis Drake, Captain Kidd, and Cruel Henry Morgan?" Also, "Why was Cruel Henry Morgan, cruel?"

DURING READING

Clarify Understanding

by using photographs, charts, and other graphics to help me understand what I'm reading.

My Thinking

This strategy says to clarify understanding by using photographs, charts, and other graphics to help me understand what I'm reading. I will stop and think about this strategy every time I come to a red button like this ⬤.

Robbers of the Seas

W hat comes to your mind when you see the word *pirate*? Swords, parrots, gold earrings, walking the plank? What about the "Jolly Roger"—the black flag showing a skull and crossbones? If so, you're not alone. Much of how we think about pirates comes from the book *Treasure Island* by Robert Louis Stevenson. Stevenson's pirates were colorful, hardhearted, sword-carrying villains. They were called swashbucklers. The buckles on their belts used to swash—or clank—when they fought.

Real pirates really did carry swords, and they kept parrots for pets. Some dressed in fancy clothes that they may have stolen. And they strapped several loaded pistols to their chests. Many pirates even wore a gold hoop earring. But what pirates looked like is only part of the story. The story of real pirates is much more complicated.

Strategy

Clarify Understanding by using photographs, charts, and other graphics to help me understand what I'm reading.

My Thinking
The pirates in this picture look like Vikings. The text also says that Vikings raided coastal towns all over Europe.

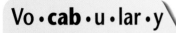

The Beginnings

Piracy has probably been around for as long as people have sailed the seas. For example, historians know that pirates sailed the Aegean Sea. They raided cities along the coast of Greece. Later, Roman warships fought pirates in the Mediterranean Sea. Those pirates stole olive oil and wine from Roman merchants.

After that, fearsome Vikings raided coastal towns all over Europe. Pirates sailed off the Barbary Coast of North Africa. They raided in the China Sea and along the coast of Brazil in South America. Anywhere there were boats with **cargo** to steal,

The Vikings were among the earliest raiders of the seas.

pirates were a danger. But the "golden age" of pirates began around 1520 in the Caribbean Sea—shortly after Europeans began exploring the Americas. Their golden age continued for hundreds of years.

The Pirate's Life

Piracy was a dangerous job. Pirates who were caught by authorities were usually executed. Even so, many pirates chose the life because it offered the chance to be free. Why did they do this? For many, piracy was better than the life they left behind. For example, many English pirates who sailed the Caribbean had first been in the navy.

Life in the navy could be miserable. In those years, sailors did not join the navy by choice. They were **conscripted**.

Vo·cab·u·lar·y

cargo (**kar**•goh)—the freight, or goods, carried by a vehicle, such as a ship

conscripted (kuhn•**skrip**•tid) —drafted

Sailors were not free to leave the navy, and conditions aboard ship were poor. The food was awful. Many sailors got terrible diseases, such as **tuberculosis** and **scurvy**. If they broke the rules, sailors could be whipped. They could even be hanged. When navy ships were raided or captured by pirates, many sailors were happy to join pirate crews.

However, life aboard pirate ships was not much better than on navy ships. Every pirate ship had a large number of rats. They could chew their way right through the boat. The holes they made sometimes sank the ship! The rats also helped themselves to food that was meant to feed the crew. The food was not fancy fare, however. Sometimes, fresh fish was available. When it wasn't, the men survived on bug-infested biscuits and dried meat.

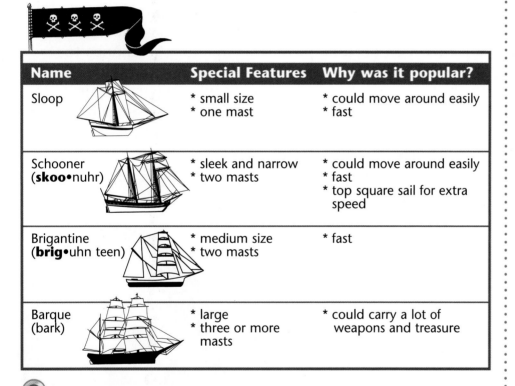

Name		Special Features	Why was it popular?
Sloop		* small size * one mast	* could move around easily * fast
Schooner (**skoo**•nuhr)		* sleek and narrow * two masts	* could move around easily * fast * top square sail for extra speed
Brigantine (**brig**•uhn teen)		* medium size * two masts	* fast
Barque (bark)		* large * three or more masts	* could carry a lot of weapons and treasure

Unlike the navy, however, pirates were very democratic. They governed themselves by written rules that covered both the captain and the crew. The rules were called "the pirate's code." For example, during a battle the captain had complete command. But in calmer times, the crew could vote about many things. And if they thought the captain was unfair, they chose someone else to be captain.

Pirates had many different types of sailing vessels. These are some of the most popular.

Vo•cab•u•lar•y

tuberculosis (tu•bur•kyuh•**loh**•sis)— a contagious disease of the lungs

scurvy (skur•vee)—a disease caused by a lack of vitamin C

Pirate crews also voted on how to divide what they stole. And they voted on whether someone had to be punished—and what the punishment should be. But that didn't happen too often. Many of the men had joined to escape the harsh treatment of the navy. So they were careful about punishing one of their own.

The pirate punishment that most people know about is "walking the plank." This involved tying up a man and making him walk blindfolded off a wooden board into the sea. The truth is, this never happened. "Walking the plank" was an invention of a nineteenth century writer. Instead, the most common punishment was called marooning. Anyone convicted of a serious offense was marooned—or stranded—on a tiny **deserted** island. Sometimes, such islands were only sandbars that vanished at high tide.

Such was the life of the pirate. Was it worth the chance to be "free"? Maybe. But there was another important reason that men became pirates. It was for the chance to become rich—and some pirates became very rich. Francis Drake is one example of someone who became a pirate to gain treasure. He succeeded—with the help of a queen.

Pirates actually never made people "walk the plank."

Francis Drake: "The Dragon"

Sometimes, kings and queens hired pirates to work for them. Such hired pirates were called **privateers**. In the late 1500s, Francis Drake was hired by the English Queen, Elizabeth I. At the time, England was in a war with Spain. The queen hired Drake to **loot** Spanish ships and settlements in the Americas. Drake's mission was a secret. No one was to know that he was working for the Queen of England.

The Spanish already knew of Drake, and they were afraid of him. They called him *El Draque*—"the Dragon." Soon, the Spanish would have even more reason to fear him.

Drake sailed all the way around the tip of South America. That is one of

Sir Francis Drake

Queen Elizabeth I knights Francis Drake in 1581.

the most dangerous places in the world for ships. The waters there are icy and rough. Drake's fleet made it through to the Pacific Ocean. But then they were hit with the worst storm they had ever seen. One of the supply ships was sunk. Another ship became separated from the fleet. Its captain sailed back to England. He reported that Drake's ship had sunk. But Drake was very much alive. He began looting along the west coast of South America, seizing huge amounts of Spanish silver and gold.

Next, Drake heard about a great Spanish treasure ship. He began searching for it and spotted the ship near the **equator**. Drake could have fought the Spaniards, but he decided to trick them. He threw a line of empty barrels overboard. He kept the barrels attached to his ship. When the barrels filled with water, they acted like brakes and slowed Drake's ship down. To the Spanish, it looked like a loaded cargo ship.

The Spanish captain turned to greet this odd stranger. When he hailed Drake's ship, Drake quickly showed his cannons. He demanded that the other captain "strike his colors"—or lower his country's flag. This was a sign of surrender. The Spanish captain refused, so Drake and his crew attacked.

Drake's **ferocious** pirates overwhelmed the Spaniards and looted the ship. It carried 13 chests of silver coins, 26 tons of silver bars, and 80 pounds of gold. Drake's crew also found jewels, food, wine, and other valuables. The entire haul was worth more than $108 million in today's money!

Content with the treasure, Drake let the Spanish captain and his men sail away. Now Drake knew that the Spanish navy would be watching for his ship. So instead of sailing east, back to England, Drake turned west. In doing so, he sailed around the world. Drake arrived back in London on September 26, 1580. Queen Elizabeth I declared him a knight, and he was known thereafter as Sir Francis Drake. Today, he is better known as a **navigator** than as a pirate!

Strategy

Clarify Understanding by using photographs, charts, and other graphics to help me understand what I'm reading.

My Thinking
The picture on this page shows Queen Elizabeth I declaring Francis Drake a knight. Until I read this article and looked at this picture, I didn't know that pirates were hired by queens and kings to rob ships from other countries!

Vo·cab·u·lar·y

equator (i·**kway**·tuhr)— an imaginary line that circles the earth halfway between the North Pole and the South Pole

ferocious (fuh·**roh**·shuhs)— extremely fierce

navigator (**nav**·i·gay·tuhr)— a person who explores the seas by planning a course of travel

The Reluctant Pirate: Captain Kidd

Some privateers were not as successful as Drake. An example of a privateer who came to a bad end is William Kidd. Kidd had been a privateer for England before he moved to New York City. There he lived the life of a wealthy sea captain. But, he soon tired of that life and returned to England in 1695. King William of England ordered Kidd to command a ship and hunt pirates. Kidd didn't really want the job. But he wasn't prepared to argue with the King, so Kidd agreed.

Kidd and his crew began a long voyage. He had hired his crew with one condition. The crew wouldn't get paid if they didn't capture any pirate ships. But the pirates they were supposed to catch kept escaping. And, of course, so did the loot.

Finally, Kidd's crew rebelled. If they couldn't capture pirates, they wanted to *be* pirates and rob English ships. Kidd refused at first. He then decided that piracy might be the only way to keep his crew in line. So they captured a few small English ships. They didn't find much loot, however, so they took a larger ship. That one was loaded with treasure. Soon afterward, most of Kidd's crew deserted, taking their shares with them.

Captain Kidd

Kidd decided to return to America, away from his life as a pirate. First he sailed to Gardiner's Island, off the coast of New York. There, he buried the remains of his share of treasure. Then he sailed to Boston, where he hoped to regain a respectable life.

But as soon as Kidd arrived in Boston, he was placed in chains. "Captain Kidd," as he was called, was found guilty of piracy. In 1701, he was hanged in London. Kidd's body was covered in tar. He was

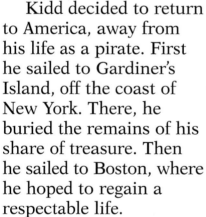

Captain Kidd burying his treasure

left hanging on the **gallows** along the Thames River for many years—as a warning to would-be pirates.

What happened to Kidd's buried treasure? No one knows for sure. People have been digging around Gardiner's Island in search of it ever since.

Cruel Henry Morgan

A third example of a pirate who had a great desire for wealth is Henry Morgan, one of the cruelest pirates who ever lived. Born in Wales in 1635, he traveled to the Caribbean as a soldier. But once there, he joined the pirates. Before long, he was elected admiral, or commander, of a group of pirates and privateers. They were called **Brethren** of the Coast.

Pirates who sailed with Morgan had to sign an agreement. It described their rights and their duties. For example, they agreed to obey a captain's orders. They agreed not to steal from their fellow pirates, or to fight one another.

In exchange for his men's loyalty, Morgan was a fair leader. He even provided some **insurance** for his men. He paid them in pieces of eight. Pieces of eight were Spanish gold coins. A pirate who lost an eye would be paid 100 pieces of eight. The loss of both legs earned 1,500 pieces of eight. The loss of both hands was worth 1,800 pieces of eight!

In 1671, Morgan's pirate fleet attacked Panama City. They stole almost everything of value. When Morgan attacked the city of Puerto Bello, in Cuba, he tortured citizens until they gave up their money and jewels. He took 60 Spanish soldiers as prisoners. He locked them in the city's **citadel** and then blew it up.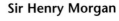

Sir Henry Morgan

Strategy

Clarify Understanding by using photographs, charts, and other graphics to help me understand what I'm reading.

My Thinking
The pirates in these pictures look exactly like what I picture pirates to look like. Since there were no cameras then, this is an artist's idea of what they looked like. I wonder how close they are to the truth. I think this is what Captain Kidd and Cruel Henry Morgan really looked like.

Vo•cab•u•lar•y

gallows (**gal**•ohz)—structures used for hanging

brethren (**breth**•ruhn)—brothers

insurance (in•**shur**•uhns)—a promise to pay a certain amount for a loss

citadel (**sit**•uh•duhl)—a fort guarding a city

Clarify Understanding by using photographs, charts, and other graphics to help me understand what I'm reading.

My Thinking
The flag of the skull and crossbones tells me which of these ships is the pirate ship. The pirate ship seems to be winning this battle.

A pirate vessel with a flag of the skull and crossbones sinks a merchant ship.

Despite his greed and cruelty, Morgan was treated as a hero in England. In 1674, King Charles II forgave Morgan and made him a knight and governor of the island of Jamaica. Unlike most other pirate captains, Morgan was not hanged. At the age of 53, he died in his bed.

Summary

For thousands of years, pirates sailed many of the world's seas. They wanted to live a life of freedom, and they hoped to become rich. They took anything they wanted from the ships that they captured.

Pirates lived by their own code, and they made their own rules. Some pirates became famous because of their deeds. Among them are Francis Drake, Captain Kidd, and Henry Morgan.

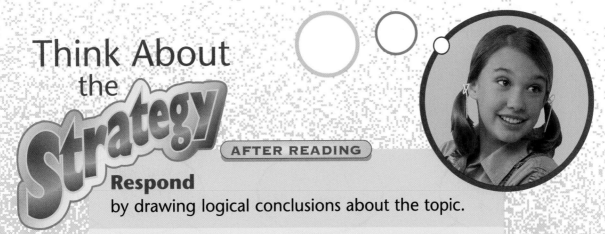

Think About the Strategy

AFTER READING

Respond by drawing logical conclusions about the topic.

My Thinking

This strategy says to respond by drawing conclusions about the topic. After reading the selection, I understand that pirates valued freedom and riches. I think that they were cruel for robbing and hurting others in order to get what they wanted. However, the kings and queens of countries who hired them were also cruel. They used pirates to take advantage of other countries and to hurt their people. The life of a pirate seemed hard. I don't think what they went through and had to do to other people would have been worth it.

Graphic organizers help us organize information we read. I think this article can be organized by using a network tree. A network tree will help me organize the main ideas of the selection. The main idea of "Robbers of the Seas" is the three robbers. I put "Robbers of the Seas" in the first bubble for the Main Idea. Then, I put the names of the three robbers in the "question" bubbles directly below. The "answer" bubbles below the question bubbles are used to give details.

Network Tree

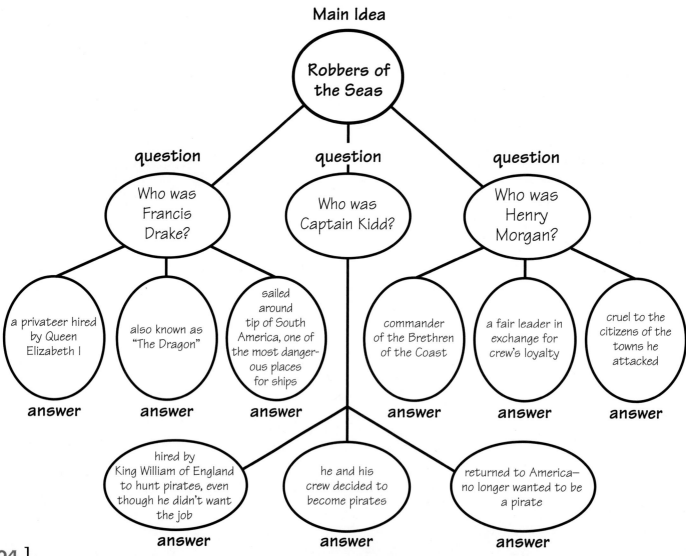

Main Idea

Robbers of the Seas

question — Who was Francis Drake?

question — Who was Captain Kidd?

question — Who was Henry Morgan?

answer — a privateer hired by Queen Elizabeth I

answer — also known as "The Dragon"

answer — sailed around tip of South America, one of the most dangerous places for ships

answer — commander of the Brethren of the Coast

answer — a fair leader in exchange for crew's loyalty

answer — cruel to the citizens of the towns he attacked

answer — hired by King William of England to hunt pirates, even though he didn't want the job

answer — he and his crew decided to become pirates

answer — returned to America—no longer wanted to be a pirate

I used my graphic organizer to write a summary of the article. Can you find the information in my summary that came from my network tree?

A Summary of
Robbers of the Seas

What were real pirates like? We can find out by learning more about Francis Drake, Captain Kidd, and Henry Morgan.

Francis Drake was a pirate who was secretly hired by Queen Elizabeth I. It was the late 1500s, and England was at war with Spain. Drake's job was to loot Spanish ships. Drake was also known as "the Dragon." He sailed his fleet of ships on a dangerous trip all the way around the tip of South America. Once Drake disguised his ship to look like a cargo ship so a Spanish ship would come close. Then Drake demanded that the Spanish captain surrender. After taking all the ship's treasure, Drake sailed around the world to escape from the Spanish navy. In 1580, Queen Elizabeth I made him a knight.

Captain Kidd began as a wealthy sea captain. King William of England hired Kidd to hunt pirates, even though Kidd did not want the job. When the pirates kept getting away, Kidd's crew decided to become pirates themselves. Kidd went along with them for a while. Then he sailed to America and tried to start a new life. Still, he was captured and hanged as a warning to other pirates.

Henry Morgan commanded a group of pirates called the Brethren of the Coast. Morgan was a fair leader in exchange for the crew's loyalty. Still, he was cruel to the citizens of the towns he attacked. He tortured them until they gave him their money and jewels. Nevertheless, Morgan was treated like a hero in England. King Charles II made him a knight and the governor of Jamaica.

These three pirates became rich and famous, but the lives of most real pirates were short and violent. Would you want to be a pirate?

Introduction
My introductory paragraph tells readers what they are about to read.

Body
Each paragraph has information from each of the branches of my network tree. The first body paragraph tells about Francis Drake. The second paragraph is about Captain Kidd, and the third is about Henry Morgan.

Conclusion
I concluded my paper by summarizing a little bit about the pirates.

Colloquial Names

Many things, such as diseases, plants, and animals, have two or more names. One is the formal name often made from combining Greek and Latin word parts. Others are **colloquial** (kuh•loh•kwee•uhl), or more familiar names.

As you read and come to a difficult formal name, look for clues in the sentence that remind you of the familiar name. *Colloquial* means "used in informal conversation." A colloquial name is sometimes an abbreviation of the formal name.

For example, in the selection "Robbers of the Seas," you read that pirates were often sick with diseases. One such disease was *tuberculosis*. You might know this disease by its more familiar, colloquial name. *Tuberculosis* is sometimes called *TB*.

The column on the left is a list of the formal names of some diseases along with facts about the disease. The column on the right is a list of the colloquial names of the same diseases. On a separate sheet of paper, match the formal name on the left with its colloquial name on the right. Use a dictionary if you need help.

1. **Malaria** is spread by mosquitoes and is a major health problem in Africa.
2. **Scarlatina**'s symptoms are a red rash and red nose.
3. **Varicella** usually develops once in a lifetime during childhood.
4. **Rubella** has symptoms that include red swollen bumps.
5. **Parotitis** has symptoms that include swelling of the temples and jaw area.

a. scarlet fever
b. measles
c. mumps
d. blackwater fever
e. chicken pox

Poetry

The following poem is from the classic novel *Treasure Island* by
Robert Louis Stevenson. This novel involves a buried pirate treasure,
a lost map, a hero, a villain, and adventures on the high seas.
Practice reading the poem clearly, fluently, and with good expression.

Fluency **TIP**

When reading this poem, pay particular attention to the commas and exclamation points.
Think about how one might feel in the days of pirates, treasure, and sailing adventures. Express that feeling in your voice.

From *Treasure Island*
By Robert Louis Stevenson

If sailor tales to sailor tunes,
Storm and adventure, heat and cold,
If schooners, island, and maroons
And Buccaneers and buried Gold,
And all the old romance, retold
Exactly in the ancient way,
Can please, as me they pleased of old,
The wise youngsters of today:

—So be it, and fall on! If not,
If studious youth no longer crave,
His ancient appetites forgot,
Kingston, or Ballantyne the brave,
Or Cooper of the wood and wave:
So be it, also! And may I
And all my pirates share the grave
Where these and their creations lie!

Think About
the
Strategies

BEFORE READING

Set a Purpose

by using the title and headings to write questions that I can answer while I am reading.

 Write notes on your own paper to tell how you used this strategy.

DURING READING

Clarify Understanding

by using photographs, charts, and other graphics to help me understand what I'm reading.

 When you come to a red button like this ⊙, write notes on your own paper to tell how you used this strategy.

Fearsome Females of the Seas

*A*rmed with swords or pistols, pirates leaped onto the deck *of the captive ship. The men cowered in fear of the women.* Women? That's right—some of the most cruel and fearless pirates were women. Commanding fleets of ships, shouting orders, and taking captives, women sailed pirate ships.

Pirates have existed for as long as people have sailed the seas. We know of male pirates as far back as 200 B.C. History has not always recorded the adventures of women. However, we do know some information about these fascinating females.

Around the World

There were women pirates all over the world until the twentieth century. Women sailed aboard ships with their

Vo·cab·u·lar·y

goods—things made to be sold

disguised (dis•**gyzd**)—dressed up to look like someone other than yourself

infamous (**in**•fuh•muhs)—having an extremely bad reputation

fathers and husbands. Many of these women learned to sail ships themselves. Stories are told of ship's captains becoming sick and their wives leading the ship to safe harbor. Women pirates led their ships to attack other ships, capture crews, and steal **goods**.

Women became pirates for different reasons. Some liked adventure and followed the call of the sea. Some took the place of a lost man. Some joined a husband in a life of piracy. In many cases, the women were **disguised** as men on the ships. Many of them fought, captured their share of prisoners, and were guilty of murder. Sailing at different times, in different parts of the world, these women had tales to tell.

The Terrible Twosome

Piracy was a way of life in the Caribbean during the late seventeenth and early eighteenth centuries. Two of the most **infamous** female pirates, Anne Bonny and Mary Read, made their names in this area.

Anne Bonny became a pirate to seek adventure. Anne was the fiery-tempered daughter of an Irish lawyer. She grew up in Charleston, South Carolina. Running away from home at the age of 16, she married a sailor. They went to Nassau in the Caribbean. Hanging around the waterfront, Anne met a local pirate named Jack Rackham. Jack, known as "Calico Jack" because of his bright-colored clothing, sailed his own pirate ship. Anne soon deserted her husband for Calico Jack. Jack wanted to take Anne on his ship, but women were not allowed on pirate ships in the Caribbean. To sneak aboard, Anne dressed as a boy. She soon was as fierce a pirate as any of Jack's crew. Anne enjoyed the life of a pirate and the loot it brought, too.

Anne Bonny

In 1718, Calico Jack captured a Dutch merchant ship. He decided to take a young cabin boy as a prisoner. The boy soon became a friend of Anne Bonny. Eventually, the cabin boy told Anne that he wasn't a boy—"he" was a woman disguised as a boy! This woman's name was Mary Read.

Mary Read had lived through an unusual childhood in England. Mary's mother, whose young son died shortly before Mary's birth, made a courageous decision. She decided to dress her newborn daughter as a boy. In those days, girls could not inherit money. So this disguise allowed Mary's mother to receive money from her mother-in-law to support the young "boy." By dressing Mary as a boy, Mary's mother hoped that Mary would be able to collect an **inheritance**. As Mary grew up, she liked pretending to be a boy and became a **manservant**. Later, still dressed as a boy, she joined the army. There she met and married a soldier. They were married for only a short time during which Mary lived as a woman. After her husband died, Mary dressed as a man once again and joined the Dutch Navy. On a trip to the Caribbean the ship was attacked. Its attackers were none other than Calico Jack and Anne Bonny.

Anne and Mary became a terrible twosome. Neither woman seemed to be afraid of anything. They were experts at using cutlasses, axes, and pistols. Both women continued dressing as boys, and for two years they sailed with Calico Jack. When attacking a ship, the twosome would be the first to board. More fearless than most of the crew, they often called Calico Jack a **coward**.

The British, who ruled the Caribbean at that time, were tired of the raids on ships. In 1720, they attacked Calico Jack and his crew. Anne and Mary fought against the attack but were unsuccessful. The rest of the crew was of no help. Captain Calico Jack and his crew,

Mary Read

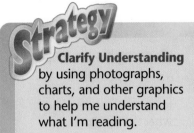
Vo·cab·u·lar·y

inheritance (in•**her**•i•tuhns) —money or property left to a person by someone who has died

manservant—a male servant

coward (**kow**•uhrd)— someone who is not brave

Clarify Understanding
by using photographs, charts, and other graphics to help me understand what I'm reading.

Write notes on your own paper to tell how you used this strategy.

including Read and Bonny, were tried in a court for robbery and murder. All were found guilty and sentenced to be hanged. When Calico Jack was taken to be hanged, once again Anne called him a coward. At the last minute, Anne and Mary were saved from hanging.

Soon afterward, Mary had a terrible fever and died in prison. No one knows what happened to Anne.

Calico Jack

Irish Queen

Some women became pirates to take the place of a lost man. Gráinne Ní Mháille is an example of such a pirate. Born in 1530, Gráinne is known in history as Grace O'Malley. She was one of Europe's most **notorious** pirates.

Grace was an Irish noblewoman. She was descended from an ancient Irish family. The family had ruled the waters of Clew Bay on the west coast of Ireland for centuries. Her father was a local **chieftain,** who raised his only daughter like a son. By the time she was a teenager, she was a skilled sailor.

The lands that the O'Malleys defended were isolated and **barren**. Life was hard. The family used their own ships to trade, to fish, and when times were bad, to raid merchant ships. They were a daring lot and sailed as far away as Spain. Grace's father took her on trips with him.

As a child, Grace lived in the family's castles at Belclare and Clare Island. She did not like to help her mother with

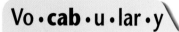

notorious (noh•**tor**•ee•uhs) —well known for bad reasons

chieftain (**cheef**•tuhn)— the leader of a tribe

barren (**bar**•uhn)—bare; unable to support crops

Clare Island

"women's work." Women's work was cooking, sewing, and taking care of the house. When she was 15 years old, Grace's father married her to another chieftain, Donal O'Flaherty. Grace and Donal had 3 children. For a short period of time, she took on the role of a wife and mother.

Grace's husband was not a dependable leader. His men soon began to look to Grace for help. She took over the chieftain's role and led ships on raids. When her husband died, Grace continued to lead his ships and men. But Irish law at that time did not allow women to be chieftains. So Grace returned to her family. Two hundred men from her husband's fleet went with her. She took over her father's fleet and made a fortune.

Grace was an excellent navigator and a bold and fearless captain. She led the 20 ships of the O'Malley fleet for over 50 years. She married again and moved to Rockfleet Castle. Braver than most men, she often called them cowards.

Sometimes Grace and her fleet attacked other chieftains. Sometimes they attacked merchant ships. During this time, England governed Ireland. The queen assigned governors to oversee each **province**. Many of these governors were soldiers who had a lot of power. They wanted to bring an end to all the attacks. This led the governors into battles with the local chieftains, including Grace. The English governor at that time sent a fleet into Clew Bay to

Vo•cab•u•lar•y

province (**prov**•ins)—a region outside of but belonging to a country

A PIRATE'S BOOTY

Gold pieces and currency	Gold was prized all over the world. Eight Spanish gold coins, called doubloons, were worth a sailor's pay for a whole year.
Silver pieces and currency	Silver coins were called pieces of eight.
Jewelry and precious stones	Pirates both sold and kept the jewelry they stole. Popular gemstones were diamonds, sapphires, rubies, amethysts, amber, garnets, and opals.
Spices and sugar	Pirates would sell this booty when they reached shore.
Anchors and rope	Pirates used stolen supplies for their own ships.
Medical supplies	Pirates suffered from many diseases. Medicine was highly valued.
Whole ships	Sometimes pirates would steal the whole ship that they were attacking. They would force the crew to join them.

 Male or female, pirates loved their treasure. This chart lists just a few examples of a pirate's booty.

capture Grace. He wanted to put an end to the pirate attacks. They were unsuccessful and were forced to turn back. A few years later, however, Grace was captured during a raid against the **Earl** of Desmond. She was put in prison for 18 months.

Grace's second husband died in 1583. According to local law, she had no right to his lands. So she went on raid after raid to defend her land. In 1592, the new governor, Richard Bingham, seized half of Grace's fleet and took her son captive. In 1593, Grace went to London to ask Queen Elizabeth I to release her son from prison. In return, Grace promised to stop her pirate raids. Impressed by another strong woman, the queen agreed. Grace's son was released. Grace was allowed to go free, and she was given a small **pension**. But Grace O'Malley couldn't resist her old ways. She continued raiding ships in the "queen's name" until her death at age 73.

Vo·cab·u·lar·y

earl (url)—a nobleman of high rank

pension (pen•shuhn)—a sum of money

The Dragon Lady

When piracy had nearly disappeared in most parts of the world, it grew in the South China Sea. Along the coast of China, women did not need to disguise themselves as men. They worked alongside their men. Women sailed and repaired boats called junks, Chinese wooden ships. Pirates were part of this seafaring life. They lived off what they took from ships at sea. When that ran out, they raided coastal villages.

Between 1807 and 1810, a lady known to **maritime** history as Cheng I Sao [ja•**ang** yee sow] became the leader of a huge pirate navy. At the height of her power, she led

Chinese pirates attacking a trade ship

2,000 armed junks, 1,000 smaller boats, and 70,000 men and women. Little is known about Cheng I Sao's childhood. The story is that when her husband Cheng I needed to choose a wife, 20 women captives were brought to him. He was already a pirate with a large fleet. Cheng I chose Cheng I Sao for her beauty. She was so angry that she tried to attack him. Impressed by her ferocity, he offered her goods to be his wife. She demanded half of all his riches and the right to help command his pirate fleet. He agreed.

Cheng I Sao created flags and fancy uniforms to make Cheng's fleet stand out. Cheng I Sao was also a skilled and cunning leader and a master at **strategy**. She took her enemies by surprise. Her ships hid in coves and behind

Vo•cab•u•lar•y

maritime (**mar**•i•tym)— having to do with the sea

strategy (**strat**•uh•jee)— planning and directing a series of actions; a clever system or plan

cliffs. **Decoy** ships were used to **lure** the enemy. Then the rest of her ships would surround the captive boat and overtake it.

Together, the couple built a huge fleet and conducted raids on ships and coastal villages. They set up a successful pirate community. Then in 1807, Cheng I died unexpectedly. One story tells how Cheng I Sao used the opportunity to become the head of the pirate community. When the pirates gathered to choose a new leader, Cheng I Sao appeared dressed from head to toe in the chief's uniform. She demanded to be named chief—and she was.

Cheng I Sao ruled her fleet like an empire. She had strict rules to keep the pirates under control. They took no prisoners, could not harm women, could not go ashore without permission, and could not take any of the loot for themselves. A financial system and a book for recording stolen goods were set up. Later, she appointed Chang Pao, a young fisherman, to lead the pirate navy. Eventually they married.

If a crew member broke Cheng I Sao's rules of conduct, the penalties were terrible. Also, her revenge on villages or captains who tried to attack her fleet was merciless. Even women and children were not spared when it came to

Using Text Features

Chart Which female pirate had a male alias? Which pirate lived during the earliest time period? Which lived during the latest period? Which pirate do you think was the most successful?

Vo·cab·u·lar·y

decoy (dee•koy)—something that attracts something else into a trap

lure—to attract

FEMALE PIRATES

Name	Aliases	Time Period	Location	Accomplishments
Anne Bonny	Ann Bonn Ann Fulford	1718–1720	Caribbean	pirate on the crew of Calico Jack's ship *Sarah Bonny*
Grace O'Malley	Granuaile	1500s	Atlantic	commanded 3 galleys and 200 men
Mary Read	Mark Read	1718–1720	Caribbean	pirated ships along with Anne Bonny and Calico Jack
Cheng I Sao		1810s	South China Sea	commanded 5 or 6 squadrons consisting of 2,000 large junks, 1,000 smaller vessels, and between 70,000 and 80,000 men and women

 Some of the famous, fearsome, female pirates of the 16th, 18th, and 19th centuries

revenge. In three years, Cheng I Sao's private fleet became far larger than any other fleet in the world.

The Emperor of China could not keep all the pirates under control. In an effort to end piracy, he made all pirates a generous offer. To any pirate who surrendered, the Chinese emperor promised a **pardon,** money, and land. Cheng I Sao finally accepted the emperor's offer. More than 17,300 members of her navy surrendered. Among them was Cheng I Sao's husband, Chang Pao. Cheng I Sao opened a gambling house and lived a relatively quiet life until she died at the age of 69.

Women of the High Seas

Female pirates like Cheng I Sao demonstrate that women were definitely not the weaker sex on the high seas. In living a life of piracy, these fearless women committed the same—or worse—crimes as their male counterparts. So the next time you think about pirates, don't just consider male pirates. Remember the likes of Cheng I Sao, Anne Bonny, Mary Read, and Grace O'Malley.

Vo•cab•u•lar•y

pardon—an official release from punishment for a crime

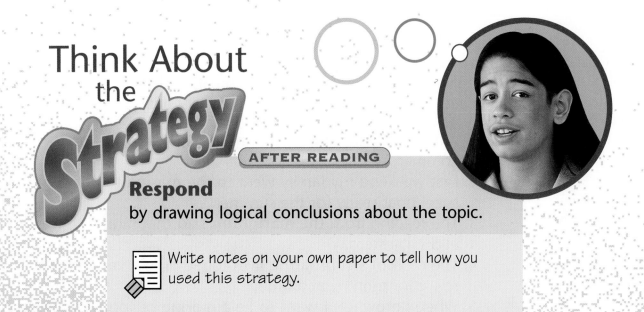

Think About the Strategy

AFTER READING

Respond
by drawing logical conclusions about the topic.

Write notes on your own paper to tell how you used this strategy.

Developing

Vocabulary

Root Words

Many words in English come from Greek or Latin **roots**. Knowing the meaning of a root can help you find the meaning of new words.

The root *mar-* comes from the Latin word *marinus*, which means "of the sea." Look at the word *maritime* in this sentence from the selection "Fearsome Females of the Seas."

> *Between 1807 and 1810, a lady known to **maritime** history as Cheng I Sao became the leader of a huge private navy.*

The root *mar-* suggests that *maritime* means "something to do with the sea." The context clues *leader* and *navy* suggest that the meaning of *maritime* includes ships and navies. So *maritime* history is the history of ships, sailing, and navigation, or all things "having to do with the sea."

Figure out the meanings of the words in boldface. Use the context clues in the sentence and the meaning of the root *mar-* to help you. Write your answers on a separate sheet of paper. Then compare your answers to the dictionary definitions.

1. When my great uncle was a **mariner,** he worked on commercial ships.
2. Last weekend my family went to the **marina** to get our speedboat ready for the summer.
3. The reading from the **marigraph** said that high tide was at 5 PM yesterday.
4. The crew of a **submarine** lives together in a very small space for months at a time.
5. When I grow up, I want to be a **marine** biologist; they get to scuba-dive all the time.

Parody

The following is a parody of the song "My Bonnie Lies Over the Ocean." A parody imitates the words or tune of another piece of work. Practice reading it out loud to yourself until you have good rhythm. Then sing it for others to the tune of the song.

TIP

If you are unsure of the rhythm, read the parody as a poem. Sing or read it with a lively voice.

Anne Bonny had wanted adventure.
Anne Bonny then looked to the sea.
Anne Bonny then married a sailor,
and she left him for piracy!

Calico Jack
Calico Jack
Said come be a pirate with me, with me.
Calico Jack
Calico Jack
We'll have adventures, you'll see!

Mary Read also wanted adventure.
Mary Read also looked to the sea.
So she dressed like a boy to be able
to live a life of piracy!

Calico Jack
Calico Jack
Said come be a pirate with me, with me.
Calico Jack
Calico Jack
We'll have adventures, you'll see!

Read 'n Bonny were fearless.
Read 'n Bonny were friends.
Read 'n Bonny together
fought hard 'til the bitter end!

Calico Jack
Calico Jack
Said come be a pirate with me, with me.
Calico Jack
Calico Jack
We'll have adventures, you'll see!

Think About the

BEFORE READING

Set a Purpose

by using the title and headings to write questions that I can answer while I am reading.

DURING READING

Clarify Understanding

by using photographs, charts, and other graphics to help me understand what I'm reading.

AFTER READING

Respond

by drawing logical conclusions about the topic.

 Use your own paper to jot notes to apply these Before, During, and After Reading Strategies. In this selection, you will choose when to stop, think, and respond.

THE REIGN AND RUIN OF PIRACY

1911 painting by N.C. Wyeth
of pirate life

During the "Golden Age" of piracy, pirates ruled the seas. Pirates from England, Spain, France, and other European nations raided **merchant** ships off the coasts of the Americas. They stole gems, silver, and gold. They also stole more ordinary goods. Another group of pirates worked off the Barbary Coast on the north coast of Africa. The Barbary pirates came from four kingdoms—Tripoli, Algiers, Tunis, and Morocco. The Barbary pirates ruled the Mediterranean Sea. Why did piracy thrive for so many years? There were many reasons.

Heroes or Hoodlums?

Perhaps the most important reason for the success of piracy was that it was supported by government officials.

Vo·cab·u·lar·y

merchant (**mur**•chuhnt)— carrying goods for sale

Columbus's ships shown along the north shore of Cuba

The kings and queens of powerful European nations encouraged piracy—if it helped them. For example, Christopher Columbus was an Italian explorer. He sailed for Queen Isabella and King Ferdinand of Spain. In 1502, Columbus was sailing near Honduras. He came upon a large Mayan trading canoe. The boat was filled with cacao beans, jewels, and some gold. Columbus attacked the canoe and stole the jewels and gold. This was the first act of recorded piracy by Europeans in the New World. Heroic explorer or pirate? That depended on whose side you were on. To his Spanish sponsors, Columbus was an explorer. To the Maya, he was a pirate.

Spain's pirates stole treasures from other Mexican groups. Piracy against Europeans in the New World began in 1523. One **monarch** who encouraged such piracy was Queen Elizabeth I of England.

In the 1580s, Spain was more powerful than England. It was taking over more and more territory in the Americas. Queen Elizabeth wanted England to set up colonies in the rich new land. Elizabeth felt threatened by Spain's power. But she couldn't afford to attack Spain. So Elizabeth secretly hired a slave trader, John Hawkins, to do the job for her. Hawkins became Queen Elizabeth's hired pirate, or privateer. At her command, he attacked Spanish ships that were carrying riches from the New

Vo·cab·u·lar·y

monarch—a king or queen

World. Hero or pirate? To the Spanish, he was just another pirate. But Hawkins became a hero in England.

Sir Francis Drake is known as a brave explorer. He was the first Englishman to sail all the way around the world. But Drake had another side. He was John Hawkins's cousin. Queen Elizabeth hired Drake to raid Spanish ships. He made several trips to the West Indies to seize Spanish treasures. Explorer or pirate? The Spanish called Drake the biggest criminal on the high seas. But Queen Elizabeth made him a knight. That's how he earned the "Sir" before his name.

Desperate and Driven

The second reason that piracy did well had to do with the average pirate's former life. Many pirates had become pirates to escape a hard life. Although not glamorous, the life of a pirate meant freedom from other terrible fates. In 1720, 98 percent of the pirates in the Caribbean were **deserters** from the merchant marines or the British Royal Navy. There was little food for navy sailors and most of it was wormy and buggy. Living quarters were crowded and awful. Pirates had more rights and freedoms than sailors. And navy punishments were very cruel. More than 20 crimes in the navy called for hanging!

Queen Elizabeth (above) supported Drake's piracy. Drake's ship (below) is attacking another.

Other pirates were runaway servants and slaves from the Americas. These men came from many backgrounds—English, Dutch, French, and African.

All of these pirates had a lot to lose if they were captured. They would be sent back to the hard lives from which they had run—or worse. This fear and their will to survive made most pirates very hard to beat.

Vo•cab•u•lar•y

deserters (di•**zur**•tuhrz)— those who leave the armed forces without permission

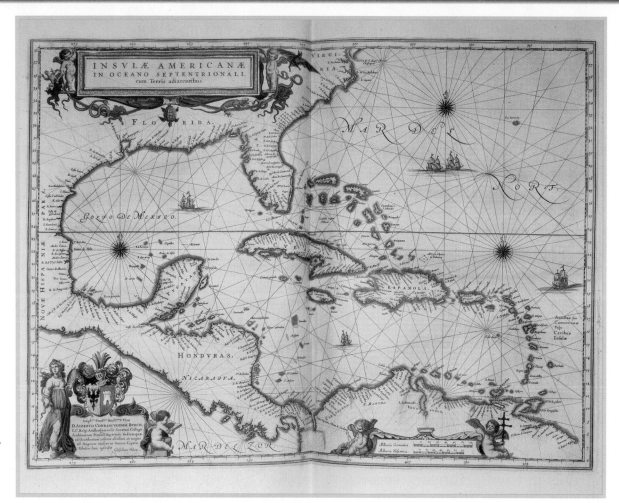

17th-century map of Central America

Speed and Surprise

Some of the reasons that piracy was so successful had to do with **geography**. Many pirates lived on the islands in the Caribbean Sea. The **inlets** and rocky places on these islands made great hiding places. Pirates could watch for prey from these **nooks** unseen.

Another reason for their success had to do with their equipment. When the pirates were out on the open ocean, they could see 20 miles from the top of a 100-foot mast. When they spied a ship, they could see which country it was from. They could tell where it was coming from and how much trouble it might be. Most ships were no match for the pirate ships. Pirate ships could easily outsail the cargo-heavy merchant ships. They could also outrun and outgun fleets of the British Royal Navy. These navy ships were light and fast, and they carried heavily armed and trained fighters. But the pirates usually had more ships

Vo•cab•u•lar•y

geography (jee•og•ruh•fee)— the study of continents, countries, mountains, oceans, rivers, and climates

inlets—small or narrow bodies of water along a coast

nooks—hidden places

[124]

and more men than the navy did. It was common for three or four pirate ships to attack one navy ship.

Also, the pirates fought fiercely, with lots of noise and motion. They hoped to frighten the ship's crews. They would attack carrying a cutlass (a type of sword), a pistol, and often a dagger between the teeth. Navy and merchant crews usually surrendered without a fight.

Sharing the Wealth

Another reason that pirates did well was that many people were glad to help them for a **percentage** of the loot. Rich English merchants **financed** English pirates. Even craftspeople, such as tailors and carpenters, would provide services and goods for part of the pirates' **bounty**. And ordinary people who lived along the coasts often helped pirates. They gave pirates provisions such as food. In return, the pirates gave them items that they could not otherwise get, like sugar and spices.

Some pirates got very rich from their lives of looting. They stole more than most public officials earned. Sometimes the people who protected pirates were **corrupt** public officials. For example, a governor of the English colony North Carolina protected one of piracy's worst criminals. The official's name was Charles Eden. The pirate was the legendary Blackbeard. In 1718, Eden offered Blackbeard a safe base off the American coast. In return, Blackbeard had to share his loot with Eden.

The Barbary Pirates

Around the same time that pirates ruled the seas off the Americas, the Barbary pirates ruled the Mediterranean. For 200 years, Barbary pirates had been attacking ships in the Mediterranean and off the coast of western Europe. The

Blackbeard the pirate

A pirate hide-out being unsuccessfully attacked in 1541

Vo·cab·u·lar·y

percentage (puhr•**sen**•tij)— an amount that varies according to the total amount

financed (**fy**•nanst)—gave money to support

bounty (**bown**•tee)—a supply of stolen goods

corrupt (kuh•**rupt**)— dishonest

Barbary Coast rulers would give **licenses** to pirates. The pirates were expected to attack the ships of other nations in the Mediterranean.

The main reason that the Barbary pirates were successful was because the victim nations would rather pay than fight. England and France had tried to fight the pirates. But the Barbary pirates were smart and fierce. These two powerful nations couldn't stop them. To protect their ships, these two nations agreed to pay lots of money to the Barbary Coast rulers. Such payments were called **tributes**.

In the late 1700s, Americans also paid tributes to the Barbary Coast kingdoms. Like the English and French, these Americans thought that it would be cheaper to pay the pirates than to fight them.

The pirates in the Mediterranean and in the Americas **thrived**—but not forever. When the powerful nations of the world finally decided they had had enough, they fought back.

A sample of the "Jolly Roger," a pirate flag from 1704

England Fights Back in the Americas

When the Caribbean pirates began raiding English merchant ships, England decided it was time to fight back. In 1718, England sent a fleet of warships under Captain Woodes Rogers to the Bahamas to attack the pirates. Rogers was a former privateer who had sailed around the world. In July of 1718, Rogers landed on Nassau in a small boat. He declared that he now was governor of the Bahamas. He offered to grant the pirates a royal pardon if they gave up their outlaw life. He also offered them a free **plot** of land. Rogers gave them until September 5, 1718, to surrender. After that, he would hunt down the pirates and hang them. To his great surprise, most of the pirates accepted his offer.

Vo·cab·u·lar·y

licenses (ly•suhns•es)—papers that show legal permission to do something has been given

tributes (trib•yoots)—money paid by a weaker ruler or nation to a stronger one

thrived—were successful

plot—a small area of ground

A few of the worst criminals refused to abandon their pirate ways. Blackbeard thought he was protected by Governor Eden. He continued to attack ships up and down America's east coast. Two years later, however, Blackbeard was dead. He had been hunted down and defeated by the British Royal Navy. Within a few months, more than 100 other pirates had been killed. The "Golden Age" of piracy in the Americas was over.

The U.S. Fights Back in the Mediterranean

By 1800, the United States was paying about 2 million dollars a year in tributes to the Barbary pirates. When the ruler of Tripoli demanded even more, the U.S. government refused to pay. Tripoli declared war.

The Americans had recently formed a small but powerful navy. It had a 44-gun ship, the U.S.S. *Constitution*, and a 35-gun ship, the U.S.S. *Philadelphia*. On October 31, 1803, the *Philadelphia* chased the pirate ship *Tripolitan*. The *Tripolitan*

The deck of the U.S.S. frigate *Constitution* while in battle

was headed for port in Tripoli. Geography had helped the pirates of the Caribbean to succeed, and geography helped the Barbary pirates, too. In the open sea, the *Philadelphia* could have caught the *Tripolitan* easily. But the approaches to Tripoli harbor are shallow, and the *Philadelphia* ran aground. The pirates captured the *Philadelphia*, and its captain was forced to surrender.

The Barbary pirates now had a ship nearly as powerful as any in the American navy. The commander of the *Constitution* realized that he would have to destroy the *Philadelphia*. The man chosen for this adventure was 25-year-old Lieutenant Stephen Decatur.

Lieutenant Decatur

The *Philadelphia* was anchored in Tripoli harbor. It was surrounded by 115 heavy cannons and 25,000 pirates. Decatur had only 74 American volunteers. On the night of February 16, 1804, Decatur took a captured pirate ship, the *Intrepid,* and sailed quietly into Tripoli harbor. When the *Intrepid* bumped against the side of the *Philadelphia,* a sailor aboard cried, "Americano! Americano!"

Decatur shouted, "Board!" His own tiny crew leaped onto the *Philadelphia's* deck. Twenty pirates were killed in the first attack. Many others leaped overboard to escape the Americans.

Decatur worked quickly. Small groups ran through the ship, leaving gunpowder and kerosene. Then they threw a torch. Decatur was the last to leave the *Philadelphia.* He made a running leap onto the deck of the *Intrepid* just as the *Philadelphia* burst into flames. The fires aboard the *Philadelphia* lit up the harbor. Then it exploded like a volcano, sending timber and tar skyward. It was only one ship and 20 pirates, but its loss meant that piracy's **foothold** in the Mediterranean was weakening.

The final battle of the Barbary war took place on land in 1805. William Eaton led the way. Eaton was America's representative to the Barbary states. As representative, he was outraged by the tribute that he had to pay to the pirates who ran the Barbary states. Eaton led an army that also included about 400 Greek, Arab, and Turkish soldiers—and more than 100 camels. They marched 500

The captured American ship *Philadelphia* was burned by Stephen Decatur and his crew in Tripoli harbor in 1804.

Vo·cab·u·lar·y

foothold—a firm position

miles over the North African desert and captured the city of Derna, in Tripoli.

The troops, led by the U.S. Marines, charged against the city's walls. They were victorious! The young American nation had finally done what the older, larger European nations couldn't do. It had stopped the Barbary pirates. For hundreds of years, the Barbary pirates had attacked merchant ships in the Mediterranean Sea. Finally, the thievery and **treachery** of the pirates were coming to an end.

William Eaton and an army were led by the U.S. Marines to capture Derna, a seaport of Tripoli.

Piracy's Long-Lasting Effects

Love of the pirate lore has continued into the twenty-first century. Many books and movies have been written about this exciting time period. However, more than just show business was changed by these daring men and women. Piracy did have positive, historical effects. Pirates brought trade to struggling British, French, and Dutch colonies. Until this time, only the Spanish had a hold on the Americas. Now other colonies were able to break this barrier. International law had its roots in piracy. Because of the battles and wars fought between pirates and colonies, countries were forced to make agreements with each other.

Summary

Piracy succeeded in different parts of the world from the sixteenth century to the early ninteenth century for many reasons. In some cases, countries protected, or even sponsored, piracy. In other cases, corrupt officials were only too happy to share the bounty. Other reasons had to do with the pirates' superior ships, numbers, and tactics. Piracy finally ended in the Americas when the English had had enough. They captured pirates off the coast of the southern colonies. They also bribed the Caribbean pirates with pardons and land. After a lengthy war, the U.S. Marines defeated the Barbary pirates in the Mediterranean. The pirates may have suffered a defeat that changed their lives. However, pirates have had a long-lasting impact on the attitudes of many people and nations. The pirates' dreams of freedom and adventure will live on forever.

Vo•cab•u•lar•y

treachery (trech•uh•ree)— willful betrayal

Comparatives and Superlatives

A **comparative** is an adjective or adverb that compares two things. A **superlative** is an adjective or adverb that compares three or more things. One way to tell the difference is to look at the letters at the end of a word. Many comparatives end in the letters *-er*. Many superlatives end in the letters *-est*.

The comparative form is often followed by the word *than*. The article *the* usually comes before the superlative form.

Look at the comparative and superlative forms of the adjective *big*:
    comparative: big(g) + *er* = *bigger*
    superlative: big(g) + *est* = *biggest*

Read the following sentence from the selection "The Reign and Ruin of Piracy."

*The Spanish called Drake the **biggest** criminal on the high seas.*

The letters *-est* at the end of the word tell you the word *biggest* is a superlative. Moreover, *the* precedes the adjective. The sentence is comparing Drake to *all* of the criminals of the seas. Drake is being compared to *many* other criminals.

Read the following sentences. Decide whether the boldface words are comparatives or superlatives. Then identify what things are being compared. Write your answers on a separate sheet of paper.

1. Spain wanted to have the **greatest** power, so its officials hired pirates.
2. Officials in other countries also sought to become the **wealthiest**. They also hired pirates.
3. Sir Francis Drake was the **bravest** English explorer of his time.
4. The British navy ships were **lighter** and **faster** than merchant ships.
5. Like the English and French, these Americans thought that it would be **cheaper** to pay the pirates than to fight them.

An Account

The following is one sailor's account, or description of events, of Decatur's Raid. Practice reading this account out loud with a strong voice and good expression.

Fluency TIP

This account recalls a very dramatic scene from Lieutenant Decatur's raid. Make your voice as dramatic as possible when you read this account of bravery and daring.

Decatur's Raid

It was the 16th of February in 1804—a night so dark it was nearly black. A group of us followed Lieutenant Decatur onto the small ketch called *Intrepid*. Our heads were covered in hoods. We did this so we would look like the Moorish pirates and not ourselves. We slipped into the harbor of Tripoli.

We drifted closer and closer to our target, the frigate called *Philadelphia*. Suddenly, there was a call from someone there. One of us called back, "We've lost our anchor. We'll be needing some help with the chains to hold us steady!"

We were lying, of course. And it didn't work. One of our enemies spotted our anchor. It wasn't lost at all. Then the commotion started. I heard Decatur shout, "Grapple and board!" I turned to see him jump onto the *Philadelphia*, pistol and blade in hand. We followed him and ran toward the hatches. Then came the order to "fire it." And we did. In a matter of minutes, the ship was in blazes. We jumped back across to the *Intrepid* and pulled away from the floating inferno.

List

Between 1719 and 1722, a successful pirate named Bartholomew Roberts worked off the coast of West Africa, the Caribbean, and Canada. He and his men captured more than 400 ships. Like many ship captains, Roberts wrote a set of rules, or articles, to guide his crew.

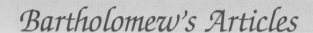

Bartholomew's Articles

1. All important decisions to be put to a vote.
2. Any man caught stealing shall be marooned.
3. All pistols and cutlasses will be kept clean.
4. No women allowed on board.
5. Any man who deserts ship in battle shall be put to death.
6. All crew quarrels will be settled on shore.
7. The captain and quartermaster to receive two shares of the booty; the master gunner and boatswain, one and a half shares; other officers, one and a quarter shares; all others, one share each.
8. Injuries to be compensated. Any man who loses a limb in battle shall receive extra booty.

Discussion Questions

Answer these questions with a partner or on a separate sheet of paper.

1. Did Roberts care what his crew thought? Explain your answer.

2. Which of these men was paid the most?
   a. the quartermaster
   b. the master gunner
   c. other officers
   d. the sailors

3. Which of these was least important to Roberts, based on his articles?
   a. his crew's ability to fight
   b. his crew's honesty
   c. his crew's happiness
   d. his crew's loyalty

4. What should a crew member do after deserting Roberts' ship during a battle?

5. Here is a list of things a crew member might do. Which one would probably upset Roberts the most?
   a. eating more than his share of the food
   b. getting in an argument with another crew member
   c. becoming injured
   d. having a different opinion than the captain

6. What was the best way for a sailor to get a bigger share of the booty?
   a. to fight bravely during battles
   b. to be loyal at all times
   c. to offer to do work no one else wanted to do
   d. to become an officer

7. Did it make sense for Roberts to forbid his crew of pirates to steal? Explain your answer.

8. What does this list of articles tell you about the men on the ship?

EXPLORE MORE

Write a Report

Research and write a report about one of the pirates mentioned in "Robbers of the Seas." Explore some of the facts and myths about this character.

Illustrate a Catalogue

Illustrate a "Pirate's Fashion Catalogue." Research some of the clothes and accessories worn by pirates between the 16th and 19th centuries. Draw the clothing and accessories, write descriptions, and give other interesting information.

Create a Pictorial Representation

Create a picture display of piracy's Golden Age. Make a map of the world to show the places where pirates thrived. Illustrate some of the famous pirate attacks discussed in this unit.

Write a Dialogue

Work with a partner to research and write a dialogue between two of the women pirates mentioned in "Fearsome Females of the Seas." The conversation can be focused on the disguises they wore, how they became pirates, why they became pirates, what their lives were like as pirates, etc.

Bake Hardtack

Pirates often went hungry on long voyages when food was scarce. One food item they ate often was hardtack. Hardtack is a hard biscuit or bread made only of flour and water. Sea biscuit is another name for hardtack. Find a recipe for hardtack and make a batch for your classmates to enjoy.

Write a Report

Research and write a report on the effects that pirates have had on history. Include positive and negative impacts.

Related Books

Blackwood, Gary. *Pirates*. Benchmark Books, 2002.

Currie, Stephen. *Pirates*. Lucent Books, 2001.

Fleischman, Sid. *The Ghost in the Noonday Sun*. Scholastic, 1986.

Harward, Barnaby. *The Best Book of Pirates*. Kingfisher, 2002.

Kallen, Stuart A. *Life Among the Pirates*. Lucent Books, 1999.

Kozar, Richard. *Infamous Pirates*. Chelsea House, 1999.

Langley, Andrew. *100 Things You Should Know About Pirates*. Mason Crest Publishers, 2003.

Malam, John. *You Wouldn't Want to Be a Pirate's Prisoner! Horrible Things You'd Rather Not Know*. Franklin Watts, 2002.

Meltzer, Milton. *Piracy & Plunder: A Murderous Business*. Dutton Children's Books, 2001.

Osborne, Will, and Mary Pope Osborne. *Pirates*. Random House, 2001.

Platt, Richard. *Pirate*. Dorling Kindersley, 2000.

Steele, Philip. *Pirates*. Lorenz Books, 1999.

Weatherly, Myra. *Women Pirates: Eight Stories of Adventure*. Morgan Reynolds, 1998.

Weitzman, David. *Old Ironsides: Americans Build a Fighting Ship*. Houghton Mifflin, 2003.

Yount, Lisa. *Pirates*. Lucent Books, 2002.

Interesting Web Sites

For more information on pirates, check out the following Web sites.

http://www.inkyfingers.com/pyrates/pyrates/index.html

http://www.nationalgeographic.com/pirates

http://www.thepiratesrealm.com

http://www.ncmaritime.org/blackbeard/default.htm

http://www.qaronline.org/history/search.htm

http://www.ukoln.ac.uk/services/treasure

Web sites have been carefully researched for accuracy, content, and appropriateness. However, teachers and caregivers are reminded that Web sites are subject to change. Internet use should always be monitored.

Strategies

Preview the Selection

by looking at the photographs, illustrations, captions, and graphics to predict what the selection will be about.

Make Connections

by comparing my experiences with what I'm reading.

Recall

by using the headings to question myself about what I read.

LEARN
the strategies
in the selection
**Challenging Mind and Body:
The New York City Marathon**
page 139

PRACTICE

the *strategies*
in the selection
**The Tour de France: World's
Greatest Bicycle Race**
page 153

APPLY

the *strategies*
in the selection
**The Iditarod: Racing for the Red
Lantern**
page 165

Think About

the Strategies

BEFORE READING

Preview the Selection

by looking at the photographs, illustrations, captions, and graphics to predict what the selection will be about.

My Thinking

This strategy says to preview the selection by looking at the photographs, illustrations, captions, and graphics to predict what the selection will be about. I see a lot of photographs of people running. It looks like they are running in races. The captions tell me about runners in the New York City Marathon and also about the Olympics. I see a map of a marathon route and also a chart of marathon winners.

I predict that this article is going to be about marathons and people who run in marathons. I will read on to see if my prediction is true.

DURING READING

Make Connections

by comparing my experiences with what I'm reading.

My Thinking

This strategy says to make connections with the article by comparing my experiences with what I'm reading. I will stop and think about this strategy every time I come to a red button like this ●.

Challenging Mind and Body: The New York City Marathon

New York City Marathon,
Verrazano Narrows Bridge

Every year, about 30,000 runners come to the "Big Apple" from all over the world. They gather to race 26.2 punishing miles through New York City. They have come to take part in the New York City Marathon. Bill Rodgers won the New York City Marathon 4 times. He has called the mass of energy at the starting line a "time bomb." But for each of the 30,000 runners, the thing they really will remember is not the start—it's what lies ahead.

Bodies Take a Pounding

A marathon is one of the most **grueling** events in sports. Win or lose, just finishing is a huge achievement. Running the entire 26.2 miles at a slow pace takes about 5 hours. That's *5 hours*—almost a whole school day—of

Vo·cab·u·lar·y

grueling (groo•uh•ling)—
exhausting

[**139**]

Strategy

Make Connections by comparing my experiences with what I'm reading.

My Thinking
I know what it is like to train. I'm on the school track team. I train every day, I pay attention to what I eat, and I have to get plenty of sleep. It is a lot of work, but I love it!

continuous running! The fastest marathon runners in the world finish in under 2 hours and 10 minutes. But this shorter time means much more effort!

Think about what it takes just to get ready to run a marathon. Runners spend months in training. They run at least 40 miles a week. That's 160 laps around a school track! Some runners run more—up to 70 miles a week. That amount of running is very hard on the body.

When people **perspire,** water leaves the body. Marathon runners perspire a lot! So, water loss during a marathon can be dangerous. Even on a cool day, runners can lose more than $2\frac{1}{2}$ quarts of water! This severe **dehydration** can damage a runner's heart and brain. That's why volunteers stand by with cups of water for the runners. They hand those cups to the runners as they pass by. And the runners try to drink as much as they can without slowing down. They also pour cups of water over their heads!

Some runners face the opposite problem of dehydration. They hydrate too much. This can lead to a condition called **hyponatremia**. This happens when drinking too much water flushes out the body's **sodium** and other minerals. It is a delicate balance. Marathon runners must constantly be aware of their bodies' reactions.

During the race, runners' feet can blister badly. Their inner thighs can bruise from scraping together. The pounding caused by running 46,000 steps, on average, begins to damage their joints. Knees and ankles can hurt for weeks. Experts tell marathoners to stop running for a certain period of time after a race is over. The hope is that they will heal enough to then start training all over again!

The New York City Marathon, 1999

Vo·**cab**·u·lar·y

perspire (puhr•**spyr**)— to sweat

dehydration (dee•hy•**dray**•shuhn)—loss of water from the body

hyponatremia (hy•poh•nuh•**tray**•mee•uh) —loss of sodium and nutrients in the body due to taking in too much fluid

sodium (**soh**•dee•uhm)— a silver-white chemical element; one of the components of common salt

Hitting "The Wall"

Marathon runners have to train carefully. If they don't train hard enough, they won't have the strength to finish the race. Marathon runners usually talk about "hitting the wall." If this happens, it usually happens to runners around the 20-mile mark. At that point, their bodies run out of energy. When they "hit the wall," runners have a choice. They either have to stop where they are or put up with a lot of pain.

Strategy

Make Connections by comparing my experiences with what I'm reading.

My Thinking
Whenever I'm working hard to finish something, it does help to visualize the end. Sometimes I think about how good I will feel when I have reached my goal.

Runners need to drink water to prevent dehydration.

If they choose to go on, runners describe it this way: Every part of your body hurts. Your lungs can't seem to bring in enough air. Your muscles are cramping. You keep thinking that you aren't going to be able to finish. You're convinced that you should quit. When you hit the wall, the race becomes a battle between mind and body. You can't finish unless you have the mental toughness to overcome the pain. Many runners can't. They end up quitting in the last few miles. Even Bill Rodgers dropped out of 5 marathons—including his first one. But many runners can finish. They push past the pain knowing they can do it. They **visualize** the finish line—and they cross it!

Vo•cab•u•lar•y

visualize (**vizh**•oo•uh•lyz)— to form a mental image of

[141]

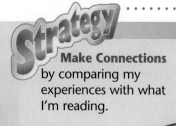
Even with all the punishment to mind and body, thousands of people run marathons every year. They range in age from their teens to their 80s. Marathon runners include people with able bodies and people with a variety of disabilities. Some people participate in wheelchairs, on crutches, and with artificial limbs. Some run without sight and hearing; others run with diseases like AIDS, **cystic fibrosis, diabetes,** and **leukemia.** Some runners make the commitment to run a marathon in order to raise money for diseases such as these and others.

All marathon participants share the same experience. They face the challenge of pushing their bodies to the limit. They endure pain that is often intense. And—except for a few of the top finishers—they work toward a goal that brings neither money nor fame. So why would anyone want to run more than 26 miles anyway? One reason could be the race's history.

The First Marathon

The roots of the marathon go back more than 2,000 years. Its name comes from a battle that was fought near Marathon, a village in ancient Greece.

In 490 B.C., the nations of Greece and Persia were fighting a war. The Persians had sailed to the Greek coast and were landing a huge army. They were met by an army of Greeks at Marathon. Even though there were 6 Persians to every Greek, the smaller army won the battle. More than 6,000 Persians were killed. The rest were forced back to their ships.

After the battle, the Greeks sent a messenger to Athens, the capital of Greece, to tell of the victory. The messenger, Pheidippides, ran 24 miles over mountains to deliver the news. Pheidippides rushed into the senate and shouted, "Rejoice! We conquer!" Then he dropped dead—or so the story goes.

It may have really happened this way. Or it may be just a legend. History books cannot agree about who the messenger was or whether he dropped dead after his run. But true or not, it makes a great story!

Vo·cab·u·lar·y

cystic fibrosis (**sis**•tik fy•**broh**•sis)—a disease that affects the mucous glands throughout the body

diabetes (dy•uh•**bee**•teez)— a disease in which the body has difficulty breaking down sugar

leukemia (loo•**kee**•mee•uh)— a disease of the bone marrow that affects the white blood cells

Birth of the Footrace

The ancient Greeks started the Olympic games in 776 B.C. But they didn't include any long footraces. That didn't start until the modern Olympics began in Athens in 1896. At the time, the leaders wanted to hold a race that would repeat the run of Pheidippides.

At first people thought that no one would want to run so far. But when a gold cup was offered as a prize, 25 runners entered the race. Twenty-one of the runners were Greek. They thought the "marathon" would be a good way to honor their country. On the day of the race, about 100,000 **spectators** lined the race route. Fifty thousand more waited in the stadium at the finish line. A Greek mailman, Spiridon Louis, won the race—and the gold cup. The marathon has been an Olympic event ever since.

The first modern Olympic games were held in Athens, Greece, in 1896.

From 24 to 26.2

So how did the current, official marathon distance of 26.2 miles come to be? The distance was changed from 24 miles to 26.2 miles at the 1908 Olympic games in London, England. The organizers of the event wanted the race to start at Windsor Castle and finish at King Edward VII's royal box at White City Stadium. In order to do this, they added 2.2 miles to the distance. The distance of 26.2 miles was made official at the 1924 Olympic games in Paris, France.

Vo·cab·u·lar·y

spectators (spek•tay•tuhrz)— onlookers, or observers, at an event

[143]

A Small Start in New York

The first New York City Marathon was held in 1970. At that time the course was made up of four 6-mile laps around Central Park—plus one lap of 2.2 miles. There were only 127 starters—126 men and one woman. Because very few people trained properly for a marathon back then, only 55 people finished. Worse, almost no spectators attended. Few people were paying attention at all.

Over the years, the New York City Marathon grew—but slowly at first. In 1971, the first woman finished the race— 19-year-old Beth Bonner. She set a record for American women at 2 hours, 55 minutes, and 22 seconds (2:55:22). Twenty years later, women would be beating Bonner's record by more than half an hour. By 1975, the race still was small. And it still took place around Central Park. That year, 534 runners entered—490 men and 44 women. They came from only 8 states, mostly from the East Coast.

Then in early 1976, America celebrated its 200th birthday. A runner named Ted Corbitt was getting ready for the New York City Marathon. Corbitt had an idea. He thought that the **bicentennial** marathon needed some "pizzazz." He suggested that there should be runners from each of New York City's 5 **boroughs**—the Bronx, Manhattan, Brooklyn, Queens, and Staten Island.

Marathon route through New York City's five boroughs

Willie Mtolo from South Africa crossing the finish line in 1992

Strategy

Make Connections by comparing my experiences with what I'm reading.

My Thinking
When we have races in my town, people in the different neighborhoods get excited when the runners pass. It's fun for the people watching. And it seems to really help encourage the runners to keep going.

When the race organizers heard the idea, they liked it. But they misunderstood what Corbitt wanted. They thought he meant that the race should be run *through* New York's 5 boroughs! The more the organizers thought about that idea, the more they liked it. They thought it might help make all of New York's neighborhoods feel a little closer to each other and to the race.

The 5-borough idea was approved and the race route was changed. The idea was a smash hit. The 1976 New York City Marathon attracted nearly 4 times as many runners as in 1975. More than 2,000 **entrants** came from 31 states and 13 foreign countries. The race has grown steadily ever since. The **field** doubled again in 1977, and again in 1978—to almost 10,000 runners. By 1993, the number of runners had grown to 30,000. In 2009, 43,741 runners lined up at the start in Staten Island.

The Growth of a Classic

The race has seen its share of great athletic moments. Bill Rodgers won four races in a row in 1976 through 1979. After Rodgers, Alberto Salazar won 3 in a row. Perhaps the greatest runner of all has been Grete Waitz, a Norwegian. She won the race 9 times, setting 3 world records in the process.

Just about everyone who runs the race notices the great support from the crowds. Hundreds of thousands of people line the race route. They cheer everyone—the last runners as well as the leaders. Some great stories result, as well. Some involve the unusual ways people have run the race. For example, in 1980, Harlem resident Ernest Conner ran facing

Vo·cab·u·lar·y

entrants (**en·**truhnts)— people who enter a competition

field (feeld)—all the participants of an event

[145]

Wheelchair contestants crossing the finish line

backwards. He finished in 5 hours, 18 minutes. That same year, Hendrick Doornekamp of the Netherlands finished in 4 hours, 27 minutes, wearing Dutch wooden shoes!

Other stories involve great personal courage or achievement. Don Bryant is a **quadriplegic**. In 1997, using only his neck muscle, Don moved his motorized wheelchair for 7 hours. In the 2003 New York City Marathon, Krige Schabort set the course record in the wheelchair division. He finished in an incredible 1 hour, 32 minutes, and 19 seconds. Cheri Blauwet finished first in the female wheelchair division. Her time was 1 hour, 59 minutes, and 30 seconds. Zoe Koplowitz has **multiple sclerosis** and diabetes. In 1998, she finished her 11th New York City Marathon in 31 hours, 10 minutes. She has become an inspiration to people throughout the world. That same year, experienced runner Jim Alexander ran with Giuseppe [juh•**sep**•ee], a blind Italian runner. They finished together in 5 hours, 10 minutes. Alexander said, "Crossing the finish line at the end, a marathon is one of those 'runner's high' experiences that seems to justify the months of training [and] sore legs . . . . Running this marathon with Giuseppe has added a whole new dimension to the experience. I expect this . . . might just be enough to get me to try it again!"

Vo•cab•u•lar•y

quadriplegic (kwod•ruh•**plee**•jik)— someone who cannot move from the neck down

multiple sclerosis (**mul**•tuh•puhl skluh•**roh**•sis) —a disease of the central nervous system

New York City Marathon Winners, 1996–2009				
	MEN	**TIME**	**WOMEN**	**TIME**
1996	Giacomo Leone (Italy)	2:09:54	Anuta Catuna (Romania)	2:28:43
1997	John Kagwe (Kenya)	2:08:12	Franziska Rochat-Moser (Switzerland)	2:28:43
1998	John Kagwe (Kenya)	2:08:45	Franca Fiacconi (Italy)	2:25:17
1999	Joseph Chebet (Kenya)	2:09:14	Adriana Fernandez (Mexico)	2:25:06
2000	Abdelkhader El Mouaziz (Morocco)	2:10:09	Ludmila Petrova (Russia)	2:25:45
2001	Tesfay Jifar (Ethiopia)	2:07:43	Margaret Okayo (Kenya)	2:24:21
2002	Rodgers Rop (Kenya)	2:08:07	Joyce Chepchumba (Kenya)	2:25:56
2003	Martin Lel (Kenya)	2:10:30	Margaret Okayo (Kenya)	2:22:31
2004	Hendrick Ramaala (South Africa)	2:09:28	Paula Radcliffe (United Kingdom)	2:23:10
2005	Paul Tergat (Kenya)	2:09:30	Jelena Prokopčuka (Latvia)	2:24:41
2006	Marílson Gomes dos Santos (Brazil)	2:09:58	Jelena Prokopčuka (Latvia)	2:25:05
2007	Martin Lel (Kenya)	2:09:04	Paula Radcliffe (United Kingdom)	2:23:09
2008	Marílson Gomes dos Santos (Brazil)	2:08:43	Paula Radcliffe (United Kingdom)	2:23:56
2009	Meb Keflezighi (USA)	2:09:15	Derartu Tulu (Ethiopia)	2:28:52

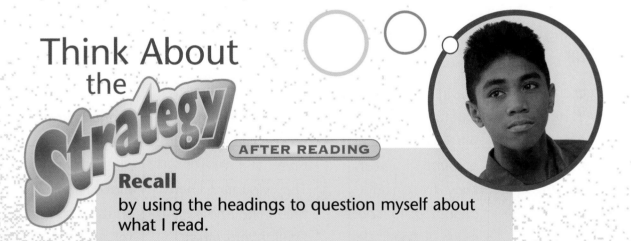

Think About the Strategy

AFTER READING

Recall

by using the headings to question myself about what I read.

My Thinking

This strategy says to recall by using headings to question myself about what I read. I will look at each heading and rephrase it as a question. If I can answer the question, then I know that I recalled and understood what I read. For example, the first heading is, "Bodies Take a Pounding." I will rephrase it like this: How do marathon runners' bodies take a pounding? I'll rephrase the heading "The First Marathon," to say: What or where was the first marathon? Using words like *who, what, when, where, why,* and *how* will help me rephrase the headings into questions. I know that I can answer these questions, because I have good recall and understanding of this article.

Graphic organizers help us organize information we read. I think this article can be organized by using a main idea table. This table organizes the information by stating the main idea of the article and then listing the details that support it. Using this table will help me organize my thoughts about how running a marathon challenges the mind and body.

Main Idea Table

Challenging Mind and Body: The New York City Marathon

Supporting Detail	Supporting Detail	Supporting Detail	Supporting Detail
Marathon runners must train hard before the race. They have to build their lungs and muscles.	Marathon runners must pay careful attention to the amount of water they drink. They cannot drink too much or too little.	Marathon runners must tell themselves they can finish the race. They visualize the finish line and think about what it will be like to finish.	Some marathon runners are sick. They have diseases that make running that much harder for them. It also makes finishing that much more special.

I used my graphic organizer to write a summary of the article. Can you find the information in my summary that came from my main idea table?

A Summary of
Challenging Mind and Body: The New York City Marathon

Completing a marathon is not easy. Running for 26.2 miles is a challenge to your mind and body. Still, thousands of people want to prove they can do it. Most know they won't win the race, but they want to finish it.

All runners must tackle the challenge to their bodies. They must prepare as well as they can for the marathon. That means training for months, building their muscles, and strengthening their lungs. Runners often train by running 40 to 70 miles a week!

During the race, runners must pay careful attention to the amount of water they drink. They cannot drink too much or too little. Even in cool weather, runners can sweat away a huge amount of water. They must drink water during the race to replace what is lost. If they don't, they will get sick and might have to drop out of the race. If they drink too much water, the chemicals in their body will get out of balance.

A marathon challenges runners' minds starting with the first day of training. However, the challenge is especially difficult toward the end of the race. That's when runners "hit the wall" and run out of energy. Their whole body hurts, and some quit. Still, many tell themselves they can finish the race. They picture themselves crossing the finish line and think about what it will be like.

Some people with certain diseases, such as AIDS, run in marathons to raise money to fight their disease. People with disabilities, some in wheelchairs, also compete in marathons. They want to prove that disabled people can do amazing things. Their friends and family members often run with them.

Running in a marathon is not for everyone. Still, many people enjoy challenging their minds and bodies.

— Introduction
My introduction tells readers what they are about to read. I'm telling my readers they are going to learn about running a marathon.

— Body
Each paragraph has information from each of the four columns of my main idea table. The first paragraph gives the supporting details from the first column. My second and third paragraphs have the supporting details from the second and third columns. The last body paragraph has the information from the last column of my table.

— Conclusion
I summarized my paper by recalling the main ideas.

Prefixes

A **prefix** is a word part at the beginning of a word. Prefixes change the meaning of the root word. Some prefixes represent a numeric value.

In the selection "Challenging Mind and Body: The New York City Marathon," you read about the *bicentennial* race. The word *bicentennial* contains two Latin word parts that have a numeric value. *Bi-* means "two," and *cent* means "hundred."

Look at the two lists below. The list on the left shows the prefixes that represent numeric values and their meanings. The list on the right shows word parts commonly combined with the number prefixes and their meanings.

Prefixes	Word Parts
uni- (one)	**-nary** (adjectives of relation)
bi-/duo- (two)	**-et** (group)
tri- (three)	**-uple** (a multiple of something)
quadra-/quart- (four)	**-ennial** (years between events)
quince-/quint- (five)	**-lateral** (number of sides)
	-cycle (wheels)

Match each word on the left with its correct meaning on the right. Use the list above to help you. Write your answers on a separate sheet of paper.

1. triennial	a. a flat shape with four sides
2. quintet	b. a vehicle that has one wheel and pedals
3. quadrilateral	c. a musical group with five musicians
4. quadruple	d. happening every three years
5. unicycle	e. to multiply by four

Parody

A parody is a song or story that is set to the tune or rhythm of another known song or story. The following poem should be read to the rhythm of Mother Goose. Practice reading the following poem fluently and with good expression. Practice reading it silently and orally.

TIP

Read this poem quickly and lightly. Read it with a joyful tone.

Willie Winkie Runs
(a parody of Mother Goose)

Wee Willie Winkie runs the marathon,

Up streets and down lanes,

Looking woebegone.

Limping toward the finish,

Gasping as he goes.

He has aching knee joints

And blisters on his toes.

Why does he do it? Why does he run?

It seems a big challenge.

It doesn't look like fun.

He says there are rewards

To push himself so far.

Most of us shake our heads

And say, "We'll take the car."

Think About
the
Strategies

Preview the Selection
by looking at the photographs, illustrations, captions, and graphics to predict what the selection will be about.

 Write notes on your own paper to tell how you used this strategy.

DURING READING

Make Connections
by comparing my experiences with what I'm reading.

 When you come to a red button like this 🔴, write notes on your own paper to tell how you used this strategy.

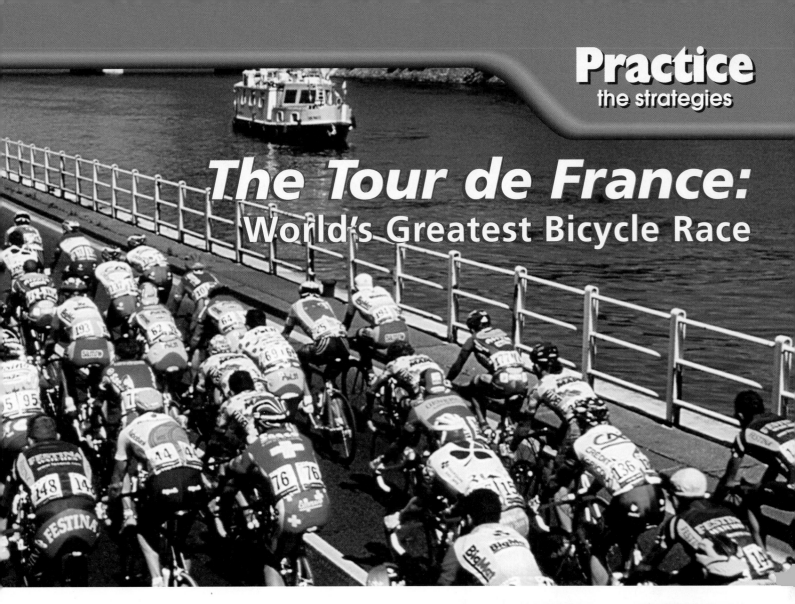

The Tour de France:
World's Greatest Bicycle Race

Think about the last time you went for a bike ride. How far did you go—around the corner to your friend's house? One mile up the road into town? Most people ride their bikes for fun, for exercise, or to get from one place to another. Imagine setting out on a ride that would take more than 3 weeks and cover more than 2,100 miles (depending on the route)! That's like going on a bike ride that starts on the East Coast of the United States and ends just a few hundred miles short of the west coast! Every year, about 200 riders set out to face such a challenge. Their ride isn't just for pleasure—it's to win the Tour de France!

Typical route for the Tour de France

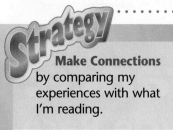
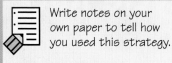
Beginnings

Long-distance bicycle racing has been a popular sport in France for more than 100 years. Riders raced from one city to the next. Then in 1903, a newspaper editor suggested a new kind of race. This race would be made up of 6 "stages," or legs. Each stage would last 1 day. All 6 stages would be spread out over 3 weeks. By the end of the race, riders would have covered about 1,550 miles. The course would begin and end in Paris and carry riders through the French countryside. The winner would be the rider with the lowest time after completing all 6 stages.

From that first race in 1903, the Tour de France was a success. People lined the streets to watch the riders speed past. They cheered loudly to encourage their favorites to continue. Maurice Garin, the winner of the first Tour de France, won a prize worth about $30,000. The race became an **annual** event. It has been run every year except for two interruptions—during World War I (1915–1918) and during World War II (1940–1946).

The Modern Tour

Today's Tour is made up of 23 stages. They include 20 road races and 3 time **trials**. Each stage is a separate race. The rider with the best time overall wins. The course is laid out to test the riders on different kinds of **terrain**—mountains, flats, and twisting roads. The shorter stages are about 124 miles. Just because they are shorter doesn't mean they are easy. Some of the most demanding stages take riders up high through the mountains. Riders who win these stages get extra points for the level of difficulty. Some of the longer stages may be as long as 217 miles. These stages are raced on flat land but demand a lot of determination from the riders. They are often faced with blistering heat. And if it rains, the riders must be extra cautious on the slippery roads.

The course weaves in and out of one town and continues on to the next. Most of it is in France, but parts may loop into neighboring countries. Towns compete for the honor of having a stage of the race pass through their streets. For that reason, the course changes every year.

Vo·cab·u·lar·y

annual (an•yoo•uhl)— happening once every year

trials (try•uhlz)—attempts that test a person's endurance

terrain (tuh•rayn)— the ground or area of land

Riders pass through the narrow streets of La Chartres.

Riders descend from the Plateau de Beille.

Strategy

Make Connections by comparing my experiences with what I'm reading.

Write notes on your own paper to tell how you used this strategy.

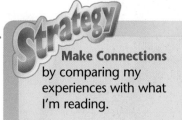

Someone once compared the Tour to running a new marathon every day for 21 days. Because this race is so grueling, it includes some rest days. On these days, riders do not race. Even with this time off, some riders do not complete the course. Usually about 200 riders begin the race, but 40 or 50 drop out. That's not surprising when you consider the mental and physical demands on the competitors. Some riders drop out due to sickness from the heat. Others are injured in crashes and are forced to stop. Muscle strains, old injuries that **resurface,** and sheer exhaustion are other race stoppers.

The Special Jerseys

Riders are racing to be the first to cross the finish line. They are also competing for other awards, including the honor of wearing one of the special colorful jerseys.

There are 5 jerseys, each **unique** in appearance. At the end of each stage, these jerseys are awarded to riders. The Yellow Jersey is the most prized. The rider with the best overall time at the end of each stage gets the Yellow Jersey. The people cheering know that the rider wearing this jersey is the current Tour leader—and one of the finest racers in the world. The next most-prized jersey is green. The Green Jersey goes to the rider with the most points at the end of each stage. The Polka Dot Jersey goes to the rider

Vo•cab•u•lar•y

resurface (ree•**sur**•fuhs)— to reappear

unique (yoo•**neek**)—one of a kind; unlike any other

The rider with the most climbing points wears the Polka Dot Jersey.

with the most climbing points. The ability to climb well is the most respected skill in riding. The Red Jersey goes to the rider with the most points for sprinting. And the first-time rider with the best time is awarded the White Jersey. Spectators look for the riders wearing these special shirts. The jersey system also helps the other riders pick out the leaders.

Teamwork

Riders in the original Tour de France competed against each other. Today, only one person wins but the race is run in teams. Each team has nine riders. It also has a support crew that consists of a trainer, a coach, and bicycle mechanics. The teams are **sponsored** by businesses that can afford the costs of supporting a team while they train and race.

Each team has a leader. The leader is the rider who has the best chance of winning a stage or the whole race. Team riders do everything they can to help the team leader win. Team riders are specialists. One may be the best climber. Another may be very fast on the flat and will help set the **pace**. Sometimes team members ride in a pack ahead of the leader. This blocks the wind from hitting the leader in the face. Other times, a pack will surround the leader to prevent other riders from bumping into him. They may also carry food and water, or bring instructions from the coach. Although they are helping the leader, all team members have the strength and **stamina** to finish the race. They are strong **competitors** and superb athletes.

In 1934, a team member named Rene Vietto had won three stages in the mountains. Then his teammate, Antonin Magne, broke the front wheel of his bicycle. Magne was the

Vo·cab·u·lar·y

sponsored (**spon**•suhrd)—supported financially

pace—the speed at which someone or something moves

stamina (**stam**•uh•nuh)—the ability to continue on even when tired

competitors (kuhm•**pet**•i•tuhrz)—persons or groups who compete with others; opponents

leader and wore the Yellow Jersey. Vietto took off his own front wheel and gave it to Magne. Vietto replaced his wheel when the team car arrived. He then rejoined the race. The next day, the same thing happened. Once again, Vietto gave Magne his front wheel. This time, however, the team car was late. Vietto knew he had lost his chance to win. Still, he finished the race and did very well. He came in fifth. For his sportsmanship, the crowds cheered him as loudly as they cheered Magne, the winner.

Heroes of the Tour

All winners of the Tour de France have the right to say they are the world's best. However, a few winners stand out above the others. Eddy Merckx was from Belgium. Merckx refused to hang back and wait for his teammates to set the pace. He pedaled hard from the beginning of each stage. He won the Tour in 1969 and for the next three years. In 1974, he won it again. He might have won the following year, but he was injured twice. First a spectator hit him, and he suffered a painful bruise. Then he fell and broke his jaw. But he was still able to come in second, less than three minutes behind the winner.

Bernard Hinault was a great French rider. He won the Tour four times between 1978 and 1982. Hinault planned to **retire** in 1986, but first he wanted to be in one more Tour. A young American, named Greg LeMond, was on Hinault's team. Hinault

**Belgian cyclist
Eddy Merckx**

> ## Strategy
>
> **Make Connections** by comparing my experiences with what I'm reading.
>
> Write notes on your own paper to tell how you used this strategy.

> # Vo•cab•u•lar•y
>
> **retire** (ri•**tyr**)—to stop working at one's career

Riders race past the Arc de Triomphe in Paris.

thought LeMond could win and promised to help. But when LeMond got ahead of him, Hinault tried to outrace him. The two battled through the mountains. Finally the younger man took the lead and won!

Although Greg LeMond was riding with a French team, he was the first American to win the Tour. Many Americans became aware of the Tour for the first time after LeMond's win. Everyone thought he would win again. Then he was shot in a hunting accident. It took him more than 2 years to recover but, in 1989, he was ready to try the Tour again. As the race came into its final minutes, LeMond was behind by 50 seconds. Pedaling furiously, he began to make up the time. With only 8 seconds to spare, LeMond won his second Tour!

The 1999 Tour Brings New Energy

Each Tour de France is unique, and no 2 years are exactly alike. Each year has a different course and new racers. Unexpected accidents occur, and new leaders **emerge** from the pack. In 1999, the field was wide open. The famous riders of years past had retired from racing. The Tour was anybody's race.

COUNTRY	YEARS WON
France	36
Belgium	18
Italy	9
Spain	12
USA	10
Luxembourg	4
Switzerland	2
Netherlands	2
Ireland	1
Denmark	1
Germany	1

Winning Countries, as of 2009

Vo·cab·u·lar·y

emerge (i•**murj**)—to come forth from

[158]

Lance Armstrong, a young American rider from Texas, had been in the Tour before. In the 1995 Tour, he had won one stage. At 25, he was a world champion road racer. Then he was hit with some awful news. Doctors told him he had cancer. It had already spread to his lungs and his brain. At first, Lance worried about his career. Then he realized that he might die.

Doctors operated to remove the cancer. Then for three months, Lance was given powerful drugs to kill the cancer. He lost his strength but wanted to compete again. When he was well, he started looking for a team. At first, no team wanted to support someone who had almost died of cancer. Finally, the United States Postal Service team decided to take him. They had raced in two earlier Tours, but they had never won a single stage.

Strategy

Make Connections by comparing my experiences with what I'm reading.

Write notes on your own paper to tell how you used this strategy.

Using Text Features

Chart Greg LeMond won the 1989 Tour de France by 8 seconds. What was the time of the second-place finisher? What other categories would you add to the chart?

Tour de France Facts	

Most Wins	**Five Times:**
	• Jacques Anquetil (France)
	  1957, 1961–1964
	• Eddy Merckx (Belgium)
	  1969–1972, 1974
	• Bernard Hinault (France)
	  1978, 1979, 1981, 1982, 1985
	• Miguel Indurain (Spain)
	  1991–1995
	Seven Times:
	• Lance Armstrong (USA)
	  1999–2005

Closest Race	1989: Greg LeMond (USA) wins by 8 seconds Final Time: 87 hours, 38 minutes, 35 seconds
Fastest Average Speed	1999: 25.30 mph by Lance Armstrong (USA)
Most Stages Won	34 stages in 7 races by Eddy Merckx (Belgium)
Oldest Winner	Firmin Lambot, 36 years old, 1922
Youngest Winner	Henri Cornet, 19 years old, 1904

Armstrong gave the team new energy. He hoped that the team could finally win some stages. He thought they could finish well, perhaps second. Then on July 3, 1999, Lance won the first stage, called the **Prologue** Stage, by seven seconds. He put on the Yellow Jersey for the first time. Suddenly Armstrong was a favorite to win.

Armstrong had to give up the Yellow Jersey on July 5. On July 11, he outraced the entire field in a long time trial. He won the jersey back, and he never gave it up again. As the race headed into the mountains, Armstrong showed remarkable strength. He was not known as a good climber, but he had been training hard, and now no one could catch him. Attacking constantly, he won three of the race's daily stages.

On July 25, he rode victorious into Paris. There he collected a fresh Yellow Jersey. He was awarded a check for $350,000, which he shared with his teammates. His victory, he said, was "a miracle." The man who had almost died of cancer less than 3 years earlier had won the world's greatest bicycle race!

Lance Armstrong leading the American team to victory in 1999

Vo·cab·u·lar·y

prologue (proh•lawg)— an introductory stage or period

Lance Armstrong continued to prove his strength and determination in the years to come. At the 2005 Tour de France, he became the first rider ever to win the Tour de France seven times. It's a remarkable feat that may never be achieved again.

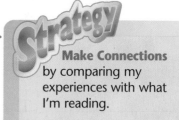

Strategy

Make Connections by comparing my experiences with what I'm reading.

Write notes on your own paper to tell how you used this strategy.

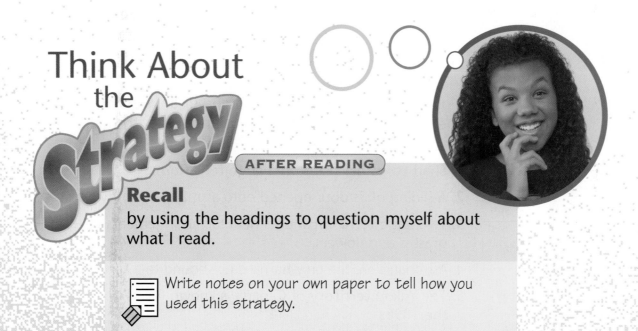

Think About the **Strategy**

AFTER READING

Recall

by using the headings to question myself about what I read.

Write notes on your own paper to tell how you used this strategy.

Vocabulary

Word Roots

Many English words come from Latin roots. Knowing the meaning of a **root** can help you find the meanings of new words.

The root *terr* is from the Latin word *terra*. *Terra* means "earth or land." In the selection about the Tour de France, you read about the **terrain** that the cyclists face.

> *The course is laid out to test the riders on different kinds of* **terrain**—*mountains, flats, and twisting roads.*

Think about what "earth or land" tells you about the meaning of the word **terrain**. Next look at the context clues *mountains, flats,* and *twisting roads.* Together, the meaning of the root *terr* and the context clues suggest that **terrain** means "ground or area of land."

Read the following sentences. Use the meaning of the root *terr* and the context clues in the sentence to help you find the meaning of the boldface word. Write your answers on a separate sheet of paper. Then check your answers with the definitions in a dictionary.

1. Shari keeps her plants in a large **terrarium**.

2. A sliding glass door opened onto a small but sunny **terrace**.

3. Two large **terra cotta** pots held tall arrangements of dried grasses and flowers.

4. Astronauts are the only humans not bound to a **terrestrial** life.

5. The Yukon **territory** of Canada is known for its gold rush in the 1890s.

6. The waters of the **Mediterranean** Sea nearly surround some countries.

7. The region where those spiders come from is **terra firm:** solid and dry.

8. Theresa's two **terriers** loved going for walks, sniffing the grass, and barking at each other.

Readers' Theater

Zayla and her Aunt Gayle are getting ready to ride their bikes. Aunt Gayle does not approve of Zayla's choice of clothes. Practice the following script with a partner.

Fluency TIP

Make your reading sound like a real conversation. Give appropriate expression to the questions and answers. Pay attention to question marks, exclamation points, and words in all capital letters.

Aunt Gayle Says "Safety Before Fashion!"

Aunt Gayle: Hey, why aren't you ready?

Zayla: I AM ready.

Aunt Gayle: I don't think so. First of all, where is your helmet?

Zayla: It messes up my hair.

Aunt Gayle: If you fall without one, you'll have a messed-up HEAD.

Zayla: Oh, Aunt Gayle. Be serious.

Aunt Gayle: I AM serious. And what is up with those bell-bottom pants?

Zayla: Don't you like them?

Aunt Gayle: Sure, but not on a bike. What do you think will happen when those bell-bottoms flap into your bike chain?

Zayla: They won't.

Aunt Gayle: I know they won't—because you're not wearing them. I mean it. Go inside and change. And while you're in there, put on some REAL shoes. You can't wear sandals on a bike. How are you going to keep your feet on the pedals? You go on . . . I'll be waiting.

Zayla: OK, Aunt Gayle. How is this?

Aunt Gayle: Are you wearing anything that will grab, snag, or tangle?

Zayla: No.

Aunt Gayle: Are you wearing shoes that will stay on the pedals and protect your feet?

Zayla: Yes.

Aunt Gayle: Now, see, I knew you had a brain in your head. Put your helmet on to protect it and let's go!

Think About the Strategies

BEFORE READING

Preview the Selection

by looking at the photographs, illustrations, captions, and graphics to predict what the selection will be about.

DURING READING

Make Connections

by comparing my experiences with what I'm reading.

AFTER READING

Recall

by using the headings to question myself about what I read.

 Use your own paper to jot notes to apply these Before, During, and After Reading Strategies. In this selection, you will choose when to stop, think, and respond.

The Iditarod: Racing for the Red Lantern

Imagine yourself standing on the back of a sled pulled by 15 dogs through the Alaskan wilderness. The wind is blowing so hard you feel as if you're about to tip over. Snow is swirling all around. Ice is stinging your face. Suddenly, the trail in front of you drops sharply. Before you know it, the sled is rushing down a hill at a terrible speed! You have to think quickly and press on the brake, slowing the sled before it runs right over the dogs! Sound like fun? Believe it or not, that's exactly what dozens of men and women do each year. The event that draws them together is the world-famous Iditarod [eye•**dit**•uh•rod] Trail Race.

The Iditarod is a sled dog race in Alaska. It takes place in March, when the Alaskan wilderness is buried in snow from raging storms. Racers and their dogs begin in Anchorage and end in the city of Nome. They travel more than 1,049 miles and cover some of the most rugged country on the planet.

The sled drivers are called mushers. *Musher* comes from the French word *marcher* [mar•**shay**], which means "to walk." Each musher rides on a sled pulled by 12 to 18 dogs. Together, they fight freezing winds, long hours of darkness, and **treacherous** hills and valleys to complete the race. Although there are many rest stops, by the time they finish, the mushers and their animals are exhausted. No wonder people say the Iditarod can't be compared to any other race!

In the 1890s, many miners set out with dog sleds to look for gold.

The Origin of Dog Sledding

In 1896, gold was discovered in Alaska. Many people rushed to the area to make their fortunes. The gold was discovered near a river that the natives called Haiditarod, which means "a far and distant place." **Miners** mispronounced the name and called it Iditarod. The miners saw the Inuit, native people of Alaska, using sled dogs. In these frigid areas, dogs with heavy coats are able to work harder than horses or other animals. It was clear that dog sledding was the best way to travel across the frozen landscape.

When the gold rush ended, sled dogs were still used to carry the mail into the coldest, loneliest parts of the state. These sled dog teams were very important to the towns-

Vo•cab•u•lar•y

treacherous (trech•uhr•uhs)— very dangerous

miners—people who remove minerals from the earth

people. They helped keep **remote** towns in contact with the rest of the world. The teams worked hard to perfect their skills. But they also took breaks from their hard work to have fun. Now and then some sledders would bring their dog teams together and have a race. These races were fun, but they played an important role, too. They helped train the dog teams to be fast. The less time that was spent out in bitter-cold temperatures, the better!

Miners heading to the river to look for gold in the1890s

The Original Iditarod

Several dog sled races are held each year. But the most famous by far is the Iditarod. The modern Iditarod race was inspired by an act of courage. During the winter of 1925, a terrible sickness was spreading through the town of Nome. The sickness could be prevented only by using a special medicine, or **serum**. If something wasn't done, thousands might die.

But no serum was available in Nome, and bringing the medicine in would be nearly impossible. It was the middle of winter, and Nome was covered in ice and snow. Winter storms made it impossible for planes to land. Frozen rivers kept boats from sailing upstream. There was only one way to reach the city—by sled dog.

The governor of Alaska asked for the best dog teams to rush the serum to Nome. At mail stations all along the route, 20 mushers and their dog teams waited for their turn to relay the serum to the next team. It could take up to 15 days to cross from Anchorage to Nome. Each day meant more people might die. The first Iditarod was a race against time.

In the meantime, a famous musher named Leonhard Seppala set out from Nome to **intercept** the serum. Seppala, along with his lead dog Togo, raced 170 miles to meet another driver and pick up the serum. Then, without resting, Seppala and his team turned back and headed for

Vo·cab·u·lar·y

remote (ri•**moht**)—located far away

serum (**seer**•uhm)—a liquid used to prevent or cure a disease

intercept (in•tuhr•**sept**)— to stop and take possession of

a village where the next team waited. Seppala and Togo covered 260 miles before handing off the serum to the next team. You may have heard of the dog named Balto. He also helped in this race and became known as a hero.

That team raced 80 more miles in blizzard conditions to Nome. The **epidemic** was stopped. This race became known as the "Great Race of Mercy."

An Uncertain Future

Gold mines closed in the 1930s, and the original Iditarod Trail was no longer used. Dog mushing dwindled by the 1950s and 1960s. But thanks to the efforts of two people, Joe Redington Sr. and Dorothy Page, the Iditarod Trail was restored.

In 1967, Alaska planned to celebrate its 100th anniversary of the state's purchase from Russia by the United States. Page was given the job of organizing this celebration. Since sled dog races were such a unique part of Alaskan history, Page proposed the idea of holding a race on the old Iditarod Trail. Joe Redington heard the idea and agreed—they would put on a race as part of the celebration.

Many people thought the idea of a dog sled race would not be popular. Also, the trail needed a lot of repair. After a lot of hard work, the race was finally scheduled. Fifty-eight mushers and their dog teams entered the Iditarod Trail Seppala Memorial Race. The race covered about 56 miles and lasted 2 days. Isaac Okleasik, from Teller, Alaska, was the winner.

Over the next few years, support for the race faded. But Joe Redington would not give up. The original race ended in the town of Iditarod. Eventually, a decision was made to extend the race all the way to Nome. That made the distance more than 1,000 miles. At first people weren't sure this would work. Who would want to enter a race that took that long? To answer that question, the committee raised a **purse** of $50,000. That was a lot of money in 1973, and it attracted much interest in the race.

Joe Redington Sr.

Vo·cab·u·lar·y

epidemic (ep•i•dem•ik)— an outbreak of a disease that spreads quickly

purse—prize money

An Amazing Return Home

In March of that year, 34 mushers started the race. Only 22 finished—the rest dropped out due to exhaustion. After 20 days, the winner of that first extended race crossed the finish line. Dick Wilmarth and his lead dog, Hot Foot, won the race.

After the race, Hot Foot somehow got loose and disappeared. Wilmarth couldn't find him anywhere. Eventually, Wilmarth had to return to his hometown of Red Devil. To his surprise, Wilmarth found Hot Foot waiting for him at home. The dog had won the race, then ran 500 miles home!

Many races have been held since that first one in 1973, thanks to the efforts of Joe Redington and Dorothy Page. To honor the pair for their commitment to dog sled racing, Joe and Dorothy were named the "father" and "mother" of the Iditarod.

The Modern Iditarod

The Iditarod has two different courses. The Northern Route is used on even-numbered years and the Southern Route is used on odd-numbered years. The length of the race is recorded as 1,049 miles, but that number is only a symbol. It's based on two things—that the race is always more than 1,000 miles long and that Alaska is the 49th state. So, although the race actually covers nearly 1,200 miles, the officials like to put the figure down as 1,049.

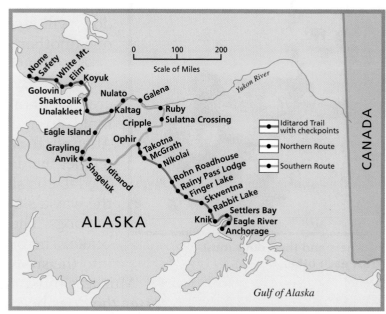

Race routes from Anchorage to Nome

Mushers and Their Dogs

Mushers and their dogs work hard to prepare for the challenge of the Iditarod. Usually, the dogs work in teams of about 15. They are connected to each other by a long harness that is attached to the sled. The sled carries the musher and all the supplies. The dogs learn to obey their driver's commands. They also learn to follow the lead dog, usually the smartest and strongest of the group. The lead dog learns to avoid dangers and to stay on the path.

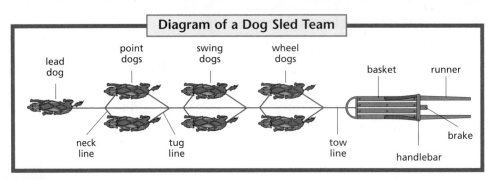

Diagram of a Dog Sled Team

lead dog · point dogs · swing dogs · wheel dogs · basket · runner · neck line · tug line · tow line · handlebar · brake

Mushers and their dogs must trust each other.

A musher spends a lot of time talking to the lead dog. This helps the dog learn to listen to its musher's voice and understand his or her commands. Although movies sometimes show drivers shouting a command to tell their dogs to "mush," that word isn't really used. When mushers want their dogs to move, they call out "Hike!" To turn right, they shout "Gee!" *Haw!* means "turn left." A driver and his or her dogs will face many dangers during a race. Trusting one another is the best way for everyone to stay safe.

Both dogs and mushers train hard. The dogs run every day. By the end of a year, the dogs will have covered 1,500 miles just in practice! Mushers train to build strength in their arms, backs, legs, and hands. After all, they don't just stand on the back of the sled and let the dogs do the work. The musher has to "pedal" the sled. This is done by pushing with one foot the way a skateboarder does. This extra "push" helps the dogs. The musher must also steer and use the brake. The brake is a pedal that pushes a hook down into the snow. This causes the sled to slow down.

Mushers must take excellent care of their dogs. Looking after the dogs becomes a **critical** matter during the race. They must be fed and watered before the mushers eat. Their beds must be properly prepared and their feet checked before the mushers rest. Many veterinarians and volunteers are available to help care for the dogs.

An Equal Race

The Iditarod is one of the only races in the world that is equal for men and women. Women do not race in a separate group from the men. They aren't given any head starts or extra help. And the truth is, they don't need it. Several women have won the Iditarod. The first woman ever to

Vo·cab·u·lar·y

critical (**krit**·i·kuhl)—very important

win was Libby Riddles. She won in 1985 by overcoming treacherous racing conditions. Since then, Susan Butcher has won the event four times!

Susan Butcher, four-time winner

Mushers face rough conditions. For that reason, they respect one another—man or woman. They will even help another racer pass them on the trail! One of the best examples of this **mutual** respect is the tradition of the Red Lantern.

During the days when dog sleds carried the mail, the mushers traveled from village to village. Because the weather was often so bad, the people at the roadhouses would hang a **kerosene** lamp outside their doorways. This lamp served two purposes. One purpose was to help the musher spot the roadhouse during heavy storms. A second, more important reason was that the burning light told everyone in the area that a sled dog team was out there somewhere in the darkness. The lamp would continue to burn until the musher arrived safe and sound.

The tradition of the lantern continues to this day. In the city of Nome, the race officials hang a red lantern. It continues to burn day and night until the last racer finally reaches the city of Nome. Then, and only then, is the lantern **extinguished,** signaling the official end of the race—until the next year, of course. Then the mushers will once again take their places behind their dogs. "Hike!"

Libby Riddles, first female winner

Iditarod Facts	
Distance	• 1,112 miles (Northern Route) • 1,131 miles (Southern Route)
Best Time	• 8 days, 22 hours, 46 minutes, 2 seconds by Martin Buser in 2002
Closest Finish	• In 1978, Dick Mackey and Rick Swenson spent two weeks on the trail and raced all the way to the finish line, where Mackey won by the nose of the lead dog by 1 second!
Prize Money	• $610,000 in prize money shared among the racers (2009) • First place earns $68,000.
Only Five-Time Winner	• Rick Swenson* in 1977, 1979, 1981, 1982, 1991 *also only person to win in 3 different decades

Vo•cab•u•lar•y

mutual (**myoo**•choo•uhl)— given and received equally

kerosene (**ker**•uh•seen)— a type of fuel

extinguished (ik•**sting**•gwishd)—put out; turned off

Thesaurus

A **thesaurus** is similar to a dictionary. It is a reference book of words in alphabetical order. But instead of listing the definitions of words, it lists synonyms (words that mean the same thing) and antonyms (words that mean the opposite).

On the second page of the selection "The Iditarod: Racing for the Red Lantern," the writer used two synonyms for the word *cold: freezing* and *frigid.* The writer might have looked for the synonyms in a thesaurus.

Sometimes writers use a thesaurus to find just the right word to convey their ideas. Other times writers use a thesaurus to avoid repeating a word.

If you look up the word *cold,* you will find the synonyms *cool, chilly, frigid, freezing, icy,* and *frosty.* You will also find the antonyms *warm* and *hot.*

Following are words from the selection with a synonym and an antonym that might be found in a thesaurus.

word	synonym	antonym
treacherous	risky	safe
exhausted	tired	refreshed
dwindled	decreased	increased

Look up the following words in a thesaurus:

walk
march
run

On a separate sheet of paper, write a list of three synonyms for each word. Then, place the synonyms in order of slowest to fastest. Discuss your answers with a partner.

Readers' Theater

It is Saturday morning at 6:00 AM in Wasilla, Alaska. It is the morning of the Jr. Iditarod Race. Jennifer, along with her parents, is getting ready for the race. Practice reading this script in groups of three.

Think about which characters would be the most excited and which characters would be worried. Then add that emotion to your part.

The Jr. Iditarod

Father (still a little sleepy): Look at you. You're ready to go. Did you even sleep last night?

Jennifer: Not much. I'm too excited. Besides, I wanted to check everything on my sled.

Mother (just coming in): Again?

Jennifer: Again. I don't want to forget anything. The race marshal will not let me run if I don't have everything on the checklist.

Father: And the dogs? How are they this morning?

Jennifer: I think they know that the race is today. They're excited, too! I'll have to ride my brake at first to pace them. If they run too fast too early, they'll wear themselves out.

Mother: You're right. It's 80 miles to Yentna Station. The dogs have to make it that far. Then you can all rest for the night.

Jennifer: And come back Sunday morning.

Father: We'll be waiting at the finish line for you. We're so proud! I knew you would do this one day.

Jennifer: I've been dreaming of this—my first Jr. Iditarod. Now that I'm finally 14, I can race. Now, let's check the sled and the dogs one more time!

Form

People who want to participate in a race often must fill out application forms. The form below is for a two-mile race for young runners. These seventh graders are raising money to buy computers for their classroom. Study the form and then answer the questions on the next page.

THE COMPUTER RACE — RUNNER INFORMATION

Date of Race: October 12
Time: 9:00 AM
Starting Line: Smithfield Middle School parking lot
Finish Line: Town Hall

First and Last Name _____

Male   Female   (circle one)   Age _____

Street address _____

City, State, ZIP _____

Phone number (___) _____

E-mail address _____

Parent's or guardian's signature _____

Emergency contact

Name _____

Phone number (___) _____

T-shirt size S   M   L   XL

(Please include $7 for your shirt with your application form.)

The fund-raising goal for our class is $5,000.

What is your own fund-raising goal? _____

Ask family members, classmates, neighbors, and others to sponsor you in the race. They can donate as much money as they choose. List your donors below.

Name _____   Name _____
Phone (___) _____   Phone (___) _____
Donation _____   Donation _____

Name _____   Name _____
Phone (___) _____   Phone (___) _____
Donation _____   Donation _____

Discussion Questions

Answer these questions with a partner or on a separate sheet of paper.

1. Kayla, age 12, is filling out this form. She lives at 14 Turtle Point Drive, Smithfield, Virginia 23431. Kayla is in seventh grade at Smithfield Middle School. Her e-mail address is kaylac@xxx.xxx. What should Kayla write on the line labeled "street address"?

2. Why does the form ask for Kayla's T-shirt size?

3. Why is the signature of Kayla's parent or guardian important?
   a. so the parent or guardian can run in the race
   b. so the school can ask the parent or guardian to help buy the computers
   c. so the parent or guardian knows when the race is and will come and cheer for Kayla
   d. so the parent or guardian knows that Kayla plans to run in the race

4. Why doesn't the form ask for Kayla's grade?
   a. This information is not important.
   b. All the runners are in the same grade.
   c. Students from different schools are in the race.
   d. This information is private.

5. Where should the runners gather at 9:00 AM on October 12?

6. The application forms have all been completed, and the seventh grade class is training after school for the two-mile run. Suddenly Kayla sprains her ankle badly. What should her teacher do?
   a. Look up her parents' phone number and call them.
   b. Send an e-mail message to kaylac@xxx.xxx.
   c. Call the person listed as the emergency contact.
   d. Take Kayla to the hospital.

7. After the race, which of these will happen first?
   a. Students will ask people to sponsor them in the race.
   b. The sponsors will pay the amount they promised.
   c. The seventh grade class will purchase computers.
   d. The seventh graders will write thank-you notes on their new computers.

8. How many computers can the students buy if they reach their goal and each computer costs $1,000?

EXPLORE MORE

Write a Newspaper Article

Research and write a newspaper report about one or two of the more famous dogs of the Iditarod. Write about how they were trained, cared for, and what they did that made them famous dogs of the Iditarod. Be sure to include photographs or illustrations of the famous dogs.

Conduct an Interview

Work with a partner to prepare an interview with one of the cyclists mentioned in "The Tour de France: World's Greatest Bicycle Race." Prepare a list of ten questions that focus on preparing for the race and participating in it. After the questions are prepared, the partners decide who will conduct the interview and who will be the cyclist. Present the interview as if it were on television for the class.

Present a Sportscast

Work with a partner to present the sports segment of the evening news. It is the long-anticipated marathon weekend in your city. Write two sports segments for each partner to present in the newscast. One segment should focus on the details of the upcoming race along with some history of the marathon. The other segment should focus on what it is like to run in a marathon.

Write a Magazine Article

This is your chance to write from the dog's point of view! Assume the role of one of the dogs of the Iditarod. Write a magazine article about what it is like being a dog of the Iditarod. Write about how you were trained, cared for, and what you felt like before, during, and after the race.

Present a Sales Pitch

Work in a group of three. Each member of the group selects one city marathon to research. Learn what makes each marathon special and attractive to runners. Each member will present a sales pitch to sell his or her city's marathon to interested runners (the class). Members of the group should be looking for characteristics such as: flat or hilly course, scenic course, neighborhood support, special city attractions, weather conditions, etc.

Research Cycling Events

Research cycling events in your state. Create a schedule showing the names of the events, where they are located, what the cycling distances are (there is usually more than one to choose from), and the registration fee. If the races are supporting a local or national charity, be sure to include that information as well. Include illustrations or graphics with your schedule. Display the schedule as if you are the director of these events and you are trying to get people excited about signing up!

Related Books

Brown, Richard. *Fitness Running.* Human Kinetics, 2003.

Fishpool, Sean. *Beginner's Guide to Long Distance Running.* Barron's, 2002.

Gutman, Bill. *Greg LeMond: Overcoming the Odds.* Raintree Steck-Vaughn, 1998.

Hayhurst, Chris. *Ultra Marathon Running.* The Rosen Publishing Group, 2002.

Henderson, Joe. *Running 101.* Human Kinetics, 2000.

Paulsen, Gary. *Dogsong.* Simon Pulse, 1999.

Riddles, Libby. *Storm Run: The Story of the First Woman to Win the Iditarod Sled Dog Race.* Sasquatch Books, 2002.

Rodgers, Bill. *The Complete Idiot's Guide to Running.* Alpha, 2003.

Savage, Jeff. *Working Out: Running.* Crestwood House, 1995.

Schultz, Jeff. *Dogs of the Iditarod.* Sasquatch Books, 2003.

Shahan, Sherry. *Dashing Through the Snow: The Story of the Jr. Iditarod.* The Millbrook Press, 1997.

Startt, James. *Tour de France/Tour de Force: A Visual History of the World's Greatest Bicycle Race.* Chronicle Books, 2000.

Stewart, Mark. *Sweet Victory: Lance Armstrong's Incredible Journey: The Amazing Story of the Greatest Comeback in Sports.* Millbrook Press, 2000.

Wilcockson, John. *The 2001 Tour de France: Lance x 3.* VeloPress, 2001.

Wood, Ted. *Bear Dogs: Canines With a Mission.* Walker & Company, 2001.

Young, Ian. *The Iditarod: Story of the Last Great Race.* Capstone Press, 2003.

Interesting Web Sites

Marathons
http://www.marathonguide.com
http://www.nycmarathon.org/

Bicycling
http://www.cyclingnews.com
http://www.velonews.com
http://www.letour.fr
http://www.roadcycling.com

Iditarod
http://www.blm.gov/ak/st/en/prog/nlcs/iditarod.html
http://www.iditarod.com/
http://www.ultimateiditarod.com/

Web sites have been carefully researched for accuracy, content, and appropriateness. However, teachers and caregivers are reminded that Web sites are subject to change. Internet use should always be monitored.

Unit 5
Strategies

BEFORE READING

Activate Prior Knowledge

by reading the introduction and/or summary to decide what I know about this topic.

DURING READING

Interact With Text

by identifying how the text is organized.

AFTER READING

Evaluate

by forming a judgment about whether the selection was objective or biased.

LEARN
the strategies
in the selection
Why Did the Dinosaurs Disappear?
page 181

PRACTICE
the *strategies*
in the selection
Continents Adrift
page 195

APPLY
the *strategies*
in the selection
Global Warming: Too Much of a Good Thing?
page 207

Think About
the
Strategies

Activate Prior Knowledge
by reading the introduction and/or summary to decide what I know about this topic.

My Thinking

This strategy says to activate prior knowledge by reading the introduction and/or summary to decide what I know about this topic.

The introduction tells us about the Tyrannosaurus rex. I have read a lot about this dinosaur. I have also seen a TV show about triceratops. I think dinosaurs are very interesting. I like reading and learning about them.

The summary tells about an asteroid that may have hit Earth and caused the dinosaurs to die. I haven't heard this before. I'll find out about it as I read.

Interact With Text
by identifying how the text is organized.

My Thinking

This strategy says to interact with the text by identifying how the text is organized. I will stop and think about this strategy every time I come to a red button like this ⦿.

WHY DID THE Dinosaurs DISAPPEAR?

A model of Tyrannosaurus rex

Vo•**cab**•u•lar•y

brachiosaurs
(**bray**•kee•uh•sorz)—big dinosaurs with long necks, nostrils above the eyes, and forelegs longer than hind legs

stegosaurus
(steg•uh•**sor**•uhs)—a dinosaur with a short neck, small head, and long hind legs

triceratops
(try•**ser**•uh•tops)—a dinosaur with a horn above each eye and a horn on its nose

Picture this. You are Tyrannosaurus rex, the greatest hunter that ever lived. You are so huge and so powerful that human beings will name you and others like you dinosaurs. The name means "thunder lizards."

You stand in the bushes, hungry. Your sharp eyes are watching the open field nearby. In the distance, you can see a few creatures with long necks. They are **brachiosaurs**. They are walking down by a lake. Should you attack? No— they are too big even for you. A **stegosaurus** appears in the distance. Its spiny back and tail do not look tasty.

Just then, another dinosaur wanders into the clearing. It has three horns on its head. Humans will call it **triceratops**. To you, it's just another meal.

You lunge forward, letting loose a mighty roar. But at the same moment, an even louder sound fills the air. A roar like a thousand **tyrannosaurs** shakes the ground. Startled, you look away from your prey and up to the sky.

A bright ball of light streaks across the sky. Smoke and flame trail behind it. The strange object disappears into the distance and slams into the ground. Seconds later, the sound of the crash reaches you. Far off, a huge cloud of dust floats into the air. It starts to spread across the sky. In a few moments, it floats across the sun. With the light blocked, day turns into night.

Your meal is forgotten. You grunt and turn away, trotting into the forest and away from the cloud. But even you—king of the great lizards—won't be able to escape it.

When Dinosaurs Roamed

Seventy million years ago dinosaurs still roamed the world. They had ruled the planet for 140 million years. They weren't very smart. But if they could think, they probably thought that they would live forever. There were too many of them. They were too strong. They would never become **extinct**.

But they did and nobody knows why. The answer to this mystery is one of the greatest riddles on the earth.

Different Theories

There are many theories, or ideas, about why the dinosaurs disappeared. Some **paleontologists** blame the disappearance of the dinosaurs on diseases. Other scientists who study dinosaurs blame it on worldwide flooding. Still others think that it was caused by aliens in flying saucers! One of the most recent theories says that dinosaurs didn't die out after all. They evolved into birds. This theory is based on some common traits found in modern birds and ancient dinosaur fossils. Scientists found that some dinosaur bones seem to be as light as bird bones.

A long time ago, all the land on the earth was bunched together.

But over time, this "supercontinent" broke apart. This event brought many changes to the earth's geography. These changes would have had a terrible effect on the dinosaurs.

Vo·cab·u·lar·y

tyrannosaurs
(ti•**ran**•uh•sorz)—large dinosaurs with small forelimbs and large heads

extinct (ik•**stingkt**)—
no longer living or existing

paleontologists
(pay•lee•on•**tol**•uh•jists)—scientists who study forms of life existing in prehistoric times

If the dinosaurs were birdlike, they might have **migrated** like birds. When the land broke apart, their patterns of seasonal movement would have been ruined. Also, inland seas would have drained into the oceans. The loss of this water would have been serious. If dinosaurs couldn't **adapt,** they would have died.

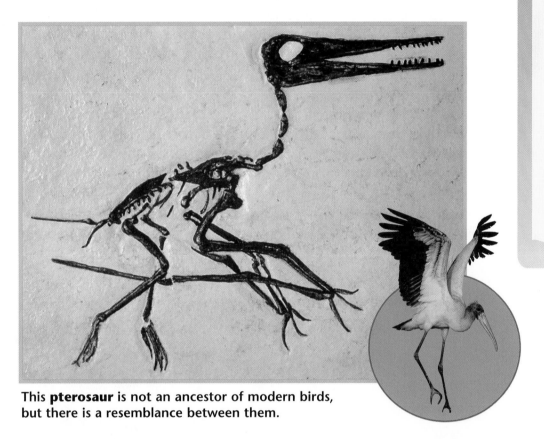

This **pterosaur** is not an ancestor of modern birds, but there is a resemblance between them.

Another idea is that *we* killed the dinosaurs. Well, not human beings, but other mammals. Some of the ancient mammals were like tiny mice. Some scientists believe these creatures were very smart. They learned how to sneak into dinosaurs' nests and eat all the eggs. Over the course of years, more of these little creatures ate more eggs. That made them stronger, and they slowly killed the dinosaurs.

A "Striking" Theory

The most popular theory about dinosaur extinction is the **asteroid** theory. This theory states that a huge object hurtling through space crashed into Earth. The impact

Vo·cab·u·lar·y

migrated (**my**•gray•tid)— moved from one region to another

adapt (uh•**dapt**)—to change to fit new conditions

pterosaur (**ter**•uh•sor)— an extinct flying reptile

asteroid (**as**•tuh•royd)—one of the thousands of small planets that orbit the sun

Strategy

Interact With Text by identifying how the text is organized.

My Thinking

I see some more cause-and-effect relationships. The eruption of Krakatoa caused a cloud of dust to circle Earth. Because of the cloud, the sun was blocked and the temperatures fell. Can you find another cause-and-effect relationship on this page?

would have sent up a huge cloud of dust that could have blocked out the sun. Scientists think that the sky would have stayed dark for months—or even years. Why do scientists think this is what happened?

Scientists support the asteroid theory by pointing to the **eruption** of Krakatoa in 1883. That volcanic eruption was huge. It could be heard almost 2,000 miles away. Darkness covered the area for a full day. A cloud of dust circled Earth. Because the cloud blocked the sun, temperatures all around the globe fell. And that was only from a single volcano! A collision with a large asteroid would have been many, many times more powerful.

Is there any proof that an object struck Earth? Is there any proof that a dust cloud blotted out the sun? The short answer to both questions is no. Scientists do know that objects from outer space have struck our planet in the past. These objects leave huge craters where they hit the ground. One of the most famous is Meteor Crater in Arizona. Twenty-five thousand years ago a meteor struck there, leaving a hole a mile wide and 600 feet deep.

Vo•cab•u•lar•y

eruption (i•**rup**•shuhn)— a sudden, violent bursting

The volcano Krakatoa erupted in Indonesia in 1883, triggering a tidal wave that killed 36,000 people.

Meteor Crater in the Arizona desert

An asteroid that could have wiped out the dinosaurs would have to have been even bigger. There are much larger craters in Canada, South Africa, and Russia. But none of them are the right age. Some scientists think that the asteroid that killed the dinosaurs may have struck in Central America. They think the crater is now hidden under the dense rain forest. Others suggest the asteroid struck the ocean. That crater would have been erased by moving water. Many theories exist.

More evidence was found in the late 1970s—thanks to a man named Walter Alvarez.

Asteroid Evidence

Walter Alvarez was a professor of **geology**. In 1978, he was studying rocks in a deep valley. Because the valley was so deep, its walls showed many layers of dirt and rock. Each layer showed a period in the earth's long history. Most of the layers were the same. They all contained tiny bits of shells left behind by forams, which are creatures that lived millions of years ago.

Vo•cab•u•lar•y

geology (jee•**ol**•uh•jee)— the study of the origin of the earth

[185]

Twenty-five different types of forams, greatly magnified

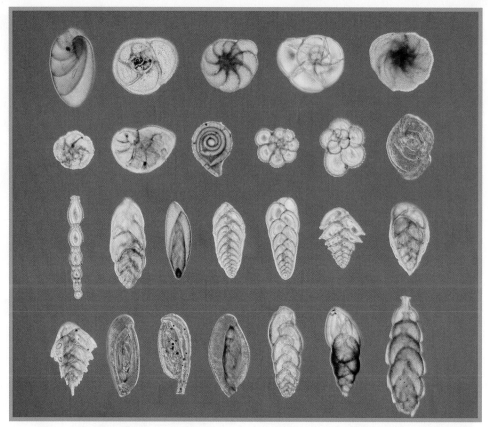

But one layer was different. It didn't contain any forams at all. And the layer that came after that layer was also different. It contained the shells of only one kind of foram. Alvarez also noticed something else. In the middle of this layer of ground he saw a thin line of clay. He took a sample to study. Working with other scientists, he learned that this line of clay was about 65 million years old. It had formed at just about the same time as the dinosaurs vanished. Also, the clay contained large amounts of a metal called **iridium**.

The metal iridium is very rare on Earth. However, it may be common in asteroids and comets that orbit our solar system.

Walter Alvarez shared his findings with his father, Luis, a famous physicist. Luis came up with the theory that 65 million years ago an enormous asteroid struck Earth. When it hit, it broke into dust and smaller bits. He proposed that it sent up such a huge cloud that the sunlight was blocked out for many months. With no sunlight, plants began to die. This caused the plant-eating dinosaurs to starve. When the herbivores were gone, the carnivores had no more meat to eat. So they starved, too. As the

Vo•cab•u•lar•y

iridium (i•**rid**•ee•uhm)— a hard and brittle metal

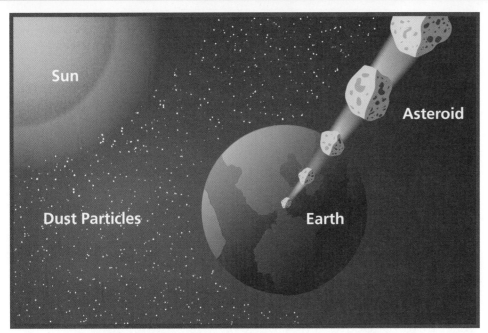

Sun

Dust Particles

Earth

Asteroid

The dust particles from the broken asteroid block the sunlight.

Strategy

Interact With Text by identifying how the text is organized.

My Thinking
There are many cause-and-effect relationships in this section:

Cause	Effect
asteroid struck Earth	sunlight blocked
sunlight blocked	plants died
plants died	plant-eating animals starved

months passed, the huge dust cloud began to settle to the ground. This dust cloud formed the layer of clay that Walter Alvarez discovered 65 million years later.

Not all scientists are totally convinced that an asteroid killed the dinosaurs. Many think that the animals' disappearance did not happen all at once. They believe that it took place slowly—over millions of years. However, most agree that it's possible. The iridium seems to be a solid piece of evidence.

More evidence was found in 1991 when the Chicxulub Crater was discovered on the Yucatán Peninsula in Mexico. This crater is also large enough to have caused extinction.

So if a huge asteroid really did smash into Earth, there are two more questions to ask. What caused it to crash here, and could it happen again?

Can Asteroids Strike Again?

The answer is yes. At least, many researchers think so. In fact, they say that asteroids strike Earth on a regular schedule. Scientists have found evidence of many mass extinctions similar to the disappearance of the dinosaurs. These disappearances of entire **species** happened on a regular basis, every 28 million years or so.

Using Text Features

Illustration Review Luis Alvarez's theory (p. 186) about what happened when a giant asteroid struck Earth. Then use the illustration on p. 187 to help retell the sequence of events to a partner.

Answer: A giant asteroid struck Earth. The asteroid broke into dust that blocked out the sun for months. Finally, the dust particles began to settle on Earth.

Vo•cab•u•lar•y

species (**spee•**sheez)—groups of plants or animals that are alike in some way

When researchers studied about 85 impact craters they found a similar pattern. They think an asteroid hit the planet once every 28 million years. But what could cause this to happen on such a regular schedule?

The answer starts millions of miles out in space. There, many asteroids float around in an asteroid belt just past the planet Mars. Another such belt, called the Oort Cloud, floats at the very edge of our solar system. Some scientists believe that our sun has a sister star that we haven't yet been able to locate. They believe it is smaller and dark. It doesn't give off enough light for us to see. This mysterious "dark star" and our sun orbit each other. Every 28 million years, the dark star comes close enough to affect the Oort Cloud. The dark star's **gravity** pulls the asteroids out of their usual path. Billions of asteroids fly across the solar system, and one of them smashes into Earth.

Right now, scientists are working hard to try to find the dark star. If they do, they may prove that an asteroid killed the dinosaurs.

Artist's conception of the asteroid belt that lies between Mars and Jupiter

Summary

Dinosaurs ruled Earth for 140 million years. Then, 65 million years ago, they mysteriously disappeared. Paleontologists have a number of theories to explain the dinosaurs' extinction. One theory, on which many scientists agree, is that Earth was struck by an object from space, such as an asteroid. The dust cloud from the strike blotted out the light and warmth from the sun. A chain of events that followed could have led to the death of all the dinosaurs. Scientists continue to look for more evidence of an asteroid crash. Until they find it, the mystery of the disappearing dinosaurs remains.

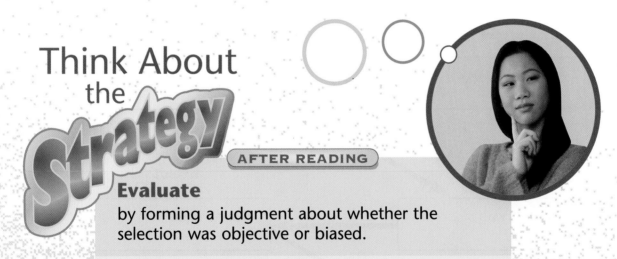

Think About the Strategy

AFTER READING

Evaluate

by forming a judgment about whether the selection was objective or biased.

My Thinking

This strategy says to evaluate the article by forming a judgment about whether the selection was objective or biased. If an author is objective, he or she is making a fair judgment and is not influenced by others. If an author is biased, he or she is influenced by others and may not be making a fair judgment.

I think the author of this article was objective. He or she gave many facts about dinosaurs and how they may have died. The author wrote about some scientific theories but used evidence to support them.

Graphic organizers help us organize information we read. A cause-and-effect chain is one type of graphic organizer. Since the text is organized showing cause-and-effect relationships, I thought this graphic organizer worked well. I started by writing a cause and its effect. Then I wrote how this effect caused another effect.

Cause-and-Effect Chain
Why Did the Dinosaurs Disappear?

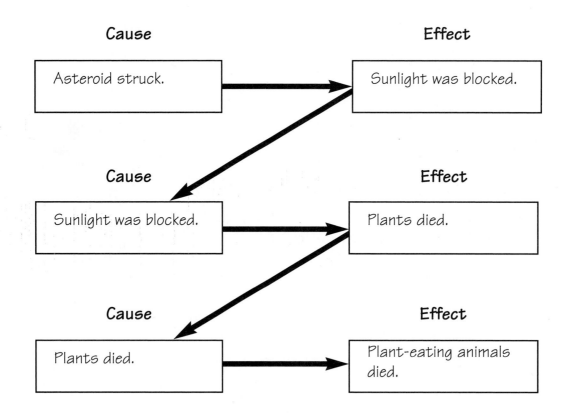

Cause	Effect
Asteroid struck.	Sunlight was blocked.

Cause	Effect
Sunlight was blocked.	Plants died.

Cause	Effect
Plants died.	Plant-eating animals died.

I used my graphic organizer to write a summary of the article. Can you find the information in my summary that came from my cause-and-effect chain?

A Summary of
Why Did the Dinosaurs Disappear?

People have many theories about what happened to the dinosaurs. The most popular theory is that an asteroid struck Earth about 65 million years ago. How can anyone be sure that this asteroid hit Earth so long ago? Scientists have found a thin layer of clay that is 65 million years old. This layer contains a metal called iridium. Iridium is very rare on Earth, so scientists think this iridium came from the asteroid. When the asteroid hit Earth, the whole process began.

Introduction
My introductory paragraph tells readers what they are about to read.

When this huge asteroid hit, it threw up a huge cloud of dust. The dust was so thick that it blocked the sunlight. The cloud might have stayed in the sky for months or years. It caused the longest night ever.

When the asteroid hit, it might have killed a few dinosaurs, but not many. However, the plants on Earth could not survive without sunlight. In time, many or most of the plants died.

The plants died, but then how did the dinosaurs die? The dinosaurs that ate plants no longer had anything to eat. They starved and died. Then the dinosaurs that ate other dinosaurs starved and died.

Body
Each paragraph has information from one row of my cause-and-effect chain.

An asteroid hit is one theory that might explain why Earth's dinosaurs died. Not everyone thinks that the impact of an asteroid explains the disappearance of the dinosaurs. Many theories are explored. Scientists will keep researching this question. Some day, we will know the answer for sure.

Conclusion
I summarized my paper by restating the main theory.

Hink-Pinks

Let's have some fun with words. A **hink-pink** is a funny question with a two-word answer that rhymes. Questions with one-syllable rhyming answers are called hink-pinks. Questions with two-syllable rhyming answers are called **hinky-pinkys**.

In the selection "Why Did the Dinosaurs Disappear?" you read about the Tyrannosaurus rex.

You are Tyrannosaurus rex, the greatest hunter that ever lived.

A hinky-pinky about the dinosaur might be:

What would you call a Tyrannosaurus rex who likes spicy food?

To solve the hinky-pinky, find a word that will be in the answer. In this case, *rex* will be a part of the answer because it is the subject of the question. Next, look for other clues. *Spicy food* is a good clue. Think about what kind of spicy food rhymes with *rex*—tex-mex. Finally, you need to make sure that both words in the answer have the same number of syllables. *Tex-mex* has two syllables. *T-rex* also has two syllables and is short for *Tyrannosaurus rex*. So, the answer to "What would you call a Tyrannosaurus rex who likes spicy food?" is a *tex-mex T-rex*.

Solve the following hink-pinks. One of the two words has been provided for you. Write your answers on a separate sheet of paper. The first two answers are hink-pinks. The next two are hinky-pinkys. The fifth one is a hinkety-pinkety. How many syllables do you think are in a hinkety-pinkety? Three.

1. What kind of tracks did most dinosaurs leave behind them? _____ trail

2. What does a small-brained dinosaur get when asked a question? _____ strain

3. What would a carnivore call a small, skinny animal? thinner _____

4. What organ did the doctor remove from the dinosaur during surgery? _____ gizzard

5. What saucy spud is a herbivore's favorite meal? tomato _____

Write your own hink-pinks. Hint: Think of the answer first.

Poetry

The following poem is a humorous poem about a dinosaur. Read this poem with much expression.

When you read this poem, practice using different tones of voice. Try to sound mean and scary. Try to sound matter-of-fact. Try to sound over-confident. Try to sound funny. How else might a T-rex read this poem?

I Am the Thunder Lizard

I am the Thunder Lizard,
fiercest of all beasts.
I roam the land each day and night
in search of fancy feasts.

The Earth it trembles 'neath my feet,
and so do lesser creatures.
They cower at the sight of me
and all my frightening features.

Running on two speedy legs
until my prey is found.
My mighty roar can shake the trees.
It's heard for miles around.

At times I wish they weren't so scared.
I'd take one as a friend.
Of course, I couldn't promise
not to eat it in the end.

Think About
the
Strategies

BEFORE READING

Activate Prior Knowledge

by reading the introduction and/or summary to decide what I know about this topic.

 Write notes on your own paper to tell how you used this strategy.

DURING READING

Interact With Text

by identifying how the text is organized.

 When you come to a red button like this ⦿ , write notes on your own paper to tell how you used this strategy.

Continents Adrift

Africa

Red Sea

Lake Tanganyika   Rift Valley   Lake Malawi

A satellite image of the Rift Valley, Kenya

Look at this map of Africa. In the east, you will see a huge new island being formed. Can you see it? You may not notice it at first. Find a place on the map called the **Rift** Valley. It starts at the narrow mouth of the Red Sea. Then follow the valley to the south. It runs for thousands of miles. You'll see two long and narrow lakes. Their names are Lake Tanganyika and Lake Malawi.

Africa is pulling apart in the Rift Valley. It's not moving very fast—less than an inch a year. But, over a long time, those inches can add up. Millions of years from now, the land east of the Rift Valley will be an island.

All over the planet, the land is changing. It may seem solid and still. But with enough time, even the most solid rock shifts and changes. Mountain ranges rise and fall. Oceans fill and empty. And even the **continents** can move.

Vo•cab•u•lar•y

rift—an opening caused by splitting; a narrow crack in rock

continents (kon•tuh•nuhnts)—the seven main land areas on the earth

[195]

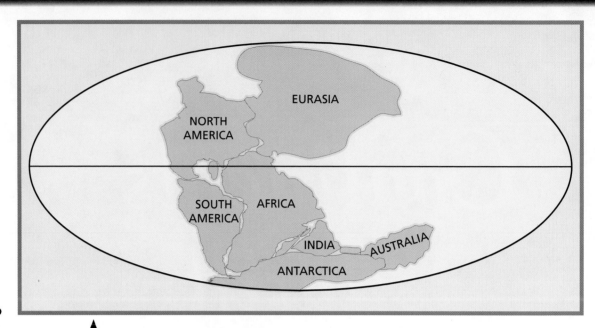

Pangaea, 200 million years ago

Using Text Features

Map With a partner, compare the map of Pangaea to a map of the continents as they are now. Take turns explaining how the surface of Earth has changed in 200 million years.

Land of "All Earth"

About 250 million years ago, most of the land on Earth was clumped together. Instead of the seven continents, there was a single large land mass. It was called Pangaea [pan•**jee**•uh], which means "all Earth." Over time, Pangaea split apart. But you still can see clues about how the continents once fit together.

Look at the east coast of South America and the west coast of Africa. They look like they would fit together—like two pieces of a puzzle. That's because the two continents were once part of Pangaea. They were pulled apart. So were North America and Europe. Asia, Australia, and Antarctica have been pulled apart, too.

Unbelievable Theories

The idea that continents are capable of moving first appeared in the late 1700s. Georges-Louis Leclerc Buffon, a French scientist, had been studying maps. He noticed the puzzle-like edges of coastlines on both sides of the Atlantic Ocean. He began to think that the continents may have once been joined together.

Buffon had the right idea. But because he had no proof, no one believed him. The same thing happened in 1915 when a German scientist named Alfred Wegener also studied maps. He too suggested that the continents had once been joined.

No one believed Wegener, either. But he made an important discovery. Wegener found that Africa and South America shared some of the same fossils. He learned that those **ancient** remains of plants and animals were all from the same era. They were all about 150 million years old. Therefore, Wegener said, the continents must have once been part of a single landmass.

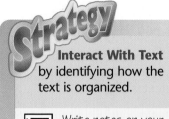

Interact With Text by identifying how the text is organized.

Write notes on your own paper to tell how you used this strategy.

Magnetic Clues

Until recently, most people thought that Earth was as solid as a crystal ball. Unlike Buffon and Wegener, they thought that the continents had been in the same place forever. After all, what force could be strong enough to move entire continents?

In the 1960s, new information made continent movement seem more likely. One clue was provided by a compass. If you hold any compass, the needle will point north. The needle is being pulled in that direction by the powerful force of Earth's invisible magnetic field. Earth is actually a huge magnet.

Rocks also can act as compasses. When volcanoes erupt, they sometimes spew lava, or hot, melted rock. As the rock cools, it hardens in place. But just before it hardens, magnetic **minerals** inside will line up with Earth's magnetic field—exactly the way a compass needle does. Scientists study these rock "compasses." The line of minerals shows where north was at the time the rock was formed.

Geologists have learned a great deal from ancient lava. They learned that Earth's magnetic field has not always pulled north. At times, over millions of years, it has reversed. Some rock formations show a striped pattern. Every other stripe points north; the others point south. One such rock formation has been found below the Atlantic Ocean. There, the rock patterns show that the ocean floor has been spreading out from a central point. Scientists say that these patterns prove that the outermost layer of the earth—its crust—has been moving slowly for millions of years.

The needle of a compass points north.

Vo·**cab**·u·lar·y

ancient (ayn•shuhnt)— very old

minerals (min•uhr•uhlz)— substances formed in the earth by nature

geologists (gee•ol•uh•jists)— scientists who study the origin, history, and structure of the earth

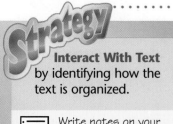

Interact With Text
by identifying how the text is organized.

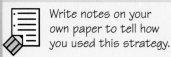
Write notes on your own paper to tell how you used this strategy.

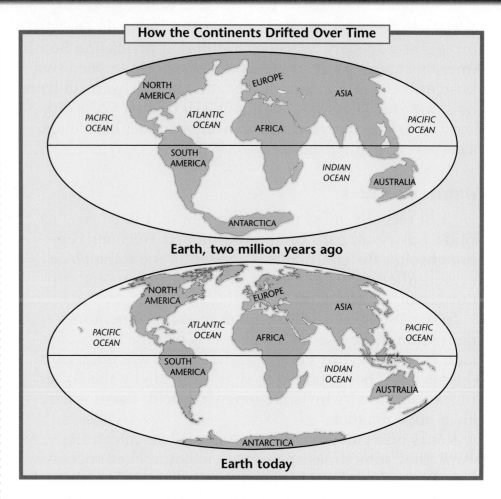

How the Continents Drifted Over Time

Earth, two million years ago

Earth today

New Ideas From New Evidence

Like chunks of ice floating in water, continents crunch together or split apart. That's because the land beneath your feet is floating, too. But it's not atop water. It's floating on a sea of **molten** rock deep within Earth. The land moves in a process known as continental drift. In 1962, geologist Harry Hess explained continental drift. The continents, Hess said, float across a "sea" of melted rock like huge ships. Earth's crust is like a cracked eggshell. The pieces of the shell are called crustal plates. Another name for these rock slabs is tectonic plates.

Scientists explain that 14 such slabs of rock cover the globe. Some are larger than others. They include dry land and ocean floor. The continents "float" above the surface of the ocean because they are made of lighter rock than the rest of the earth. The ocean floors are made of basalt, a kind of heavy rock. Basalt is much more like the material deeper in the earth.

Vo·cab·u·lar·y

molten (**mohl**•tuhn)— melted by heat

This volcanic lava has flowed onto a road and hardened.

The Moving Force

The idea that the continents are moving is now accepted. But a big question remains. What force is pushing these huge plates around? One possible answer is a force called **convection**. It's really a simple concept. To understand convection, remember that when something is heated, it tends to rise. When it's cooled, it sinks.

If you place a pot of water on the burner of a gas stove, the flame will heat the water at the bottom first. That heated water rises, and pushes away the cooler water at the top. The cool water then sinks to the bottom of the pot, where it is heated by the flame. The process goes on as long as the flame burns.

This heating and cooling—hot near the heat source, cooler at the top and on the edges—causes the water to move. Some scientists believe that the same thing happens under Earth's plates. The material being heated and cooled is molten rock. This melted rock comes to the earth's surface when volcanoes erupt.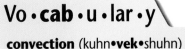

There are dozens of volcanoes on the planet that are in action and capable of erupting. They are called active volcanoes. Most of them are found around the edges of the

Strategy

Interact With Text by identifying how the text is organized.

Write notes on your own paper to tell how you used this strategy.

Convection

As water is heated in a pot, the hot water rises and pushes the cooler water down. A similar process within Earth may cause continental drift.

Vo·cab·u·lar·y

convection (kuhn•**vek**•shuhn) —the transfer of heat by motion, especially an upward motion

continents. Others are on the ocean floors. When volcanoes erupt, hot, molten rock rises. At the same time, cooler rock is sinking at other places around plate edges. All this rising of hot rock and sinking of cool rock acts the same way as the water in the pot. The plates move.

The plates move at different rates. The North American and European plates are drifting away from each other at about 1 inch per year. But the Pacific plate—the floor below the Pacific Ocean—races along at 4 inches a year. As it separates from nearby plates, molten rock rises from Earth's center to fill the gap.

While some plates are moving away from each other, others are colliding. At 1 inch or so per year, it's hard to see this movement. Over longer time periods, however, the effects can be pretty huge.

Crashing Plates

To see how this process works, take 2 stacks of a few sheets of paper and lay them flat beside each other. Then push them together. As you push, the paper will begin to bend. If you keep pushing, it will bunch up and wrinkle. The same thing happens when 2 continental plates collide.

For the past 50 million years, the Indian plate has been pushing into Asia. The land between the plates has wrinkled. Those "wrinkles" are the world's tallest mountain range—the Himalayas. The process hasn't ended, either. India and Asia still are crunching together. And the Himalayas are growing taller.

The Himalayan Mountains continue to "grow" taller.

Sometimes, when two plates bump together, one edge will sink under the other one. One plate moves up, while the other is swallowed by the earth. This type of collision can cause powerful earthquakes and create a line of volcanoes.

Strategy

Interact With Text by identifying how the text is organized.

Write notes on your own paper to tell how you used this strategy.

Other times, two plates don't collide at all. They simply grind past each other in opposite directions, like when you rub your hands together.

The San Andreas Fault in California shows what happens when plates grind together. There, a weak place in the earth's crust runs along the coast. Then it turns out to sea just south of San Francisco.

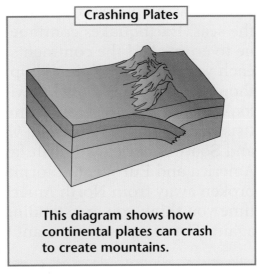

Crashing Plates

This diagram shows how continental plates can crash to create mountains.

Imagine your thumb is one plate along the San Andreas Fault; your middle finger is the other. Now hold your thumb and middle finger together tightly. Then try to slide your thumb toward your index finger. It will stick for a brief moment. When it unsticks, you'll hear the sound of your fingers snapping. That's what happens—on a much bigger scale—with earthquakes. As the two plates stick, energy builds up. The longer the wait, the

San Andreas Fault in California

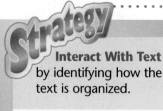
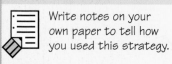
greater the energy. When the energy is released, huge blocks of land move suddenly. The greater the energy build-up, the larger the earthquake.

What Will the Future Bring?

The earth's plates continue to move—on land and under the seas. Earthquakes continue to occur. Volcanoes continue to erupt. And the continents keep drifting—by inches each year. Those inches add up to hundreds of miles over thousands of years. So what will the map of the world look like millions of years from now? This is what scientists think: Asia and Australia will be closer together. Africa and South America will drift farther apart—as will North America and Europe. California may be an island, having broken away from North America altogether! So, the next time you think you are standing on solid ground, think again. The earth is in constant transition. Can you feel it?

A volcano erupting

Summary

All over the planet, the land is constantly changing. Long ago, the continents were part of a single landmass. Scientists theorize that they have moved apart in a process called continental drift. Fourteen slabs of rock cover the globe; they are constantly moving. Scientists think that, thousands of years from now, the map of the world will look much different than it does today.

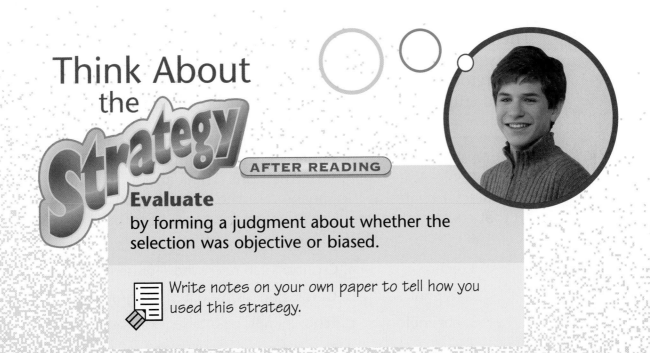

Think About the Strategy

AFTER READING

Evaluate

by forming a judgment about whether the selection was objective or biased.

Write notes on your own paper to tell how you used this strategy.

Words From Greek and Roman Mythology

You probably are familiar with some of the characters from the stories of ancient Greece and Rome. Have you heard the names of *Zeus, Hercules,* or *Medusa?* Did you know that many of the words we use today come from the names of characters from these ancient myths?

Each of these characters was known for a special trait. If you are familiar with the characters in a myth, you may be able to find the meanings of words that came from their names.

In the following sentence from "Continents Adrift," the boldface word is an example of a word that has come from a Greek or Roman mythological character.

> *When **volcanoes** erupt, they sometimes spew lava, or hot, melted rock.*

The word *volcano* comes from *Vulcan,* the Roman god of fire and craftsmanship. Some myths say that Vulcan worked in a forge underground, making tools and weapons. Sometimes his forge would erupt and spew fire and flames above ground.

On a separate sheet of paper, match the word on the left with a mythological character on the right. Think about how each character relates to the meaning of the word that comes from that character's name. Use a dictionary if you need help.

1. echo	a. **Cronos:** Titan ruler who represented time
2. hypnotize	b. **Ceres:** goddess of grain and growing
3. chronology	c. **Echo:** nymph who talked too much
4. cereal	d. **Pan:** shepherd who liked to frighten humans
5. panic	e. **Hypnos:** god of sleep and dreams
6. tantalize	f. **Tantulus:** punished by spending his afterlife neck deep in water with fruits and nuts just beyond reach

Challenge: Choose one of the characters above and find out more of his or her story. Share what you learn with your class.

Historical Description

On August 24, A.D. 79, in southwestern Italy, the volcano Mount Vesuvius erupted. The city of Pompeii was buried under ash and mud. The following is an account of how one person may have described the nearby volcanic eruption. Read the description with good expression and fluency.

Fluency **TIP**

When you read this account, try to imagine how the writer was feeling. Practice reading it as if you were telling your own story.

The Day Earth Changed

The tremors had started days before. At first they were almost gentle, like a mother rocking her little one to sleep. As the days passed, the vibrations grew stronger and lasted longer. There was a low rumbling coming from the earth.

On the afternoon of August 24th, an unusual cloud appeared over Mount Vesuvius. We could see it from our home so many miles away.

Then came the thunderous explosion. No more vibrating, but terrible shaking. It was as if Earth had been knocked out of orbit. In the distance we could see the fiery cloud bursting from Vesuvius. Within minutes, the air was filled with black smoke and rock. Everywhere was dark.

Next came the dust. It moved toward us like a dense fog. Behind it, the sky seemed lighter, but it was not the smoke lifting. It was the fire approaching. Though it stopped some miles away, its ash fell all around us. So much so that we had to shake it off again and again to keep from being crushed.

At last the cloud thinned to show real daylight. The sun was even shining. But what we saw in that light terrified us. Everything was changed and covered in ash like snow.

Think About
the
Strategies

BEFORE READING

Activate Prior Knowledge

by reading the introduction and/or summary to decide what I know about this topic.

DURING READING

Interact With Text

by identifying how the text is organized.

AFTER READING

Evaluate

by forming a judgment about whether the selection was objective or biased.

 Use your own paper to jot notes to apply these Before, During, and After Reading Strategies. In this selection, you will choose when to stop, think, and respond.

Global Warming: Too Much of a Good Thing?

You may have heard the saying "Everyone talks about the weather, but no one does anything about it." Most people *do* talk about the weather—a lot! Will it rain on your picnic? Will the sun shine for the ball game? Will it snow enough for school to close? But, what exactly is *weather* anyway? Is weather the same thing as *climate*?

Weather vs. Climate

In many places, the weather changes—a lot! One day, it may be freezing; the next, it's warm. One day the sun might shine brightly; the next day, it's hidden by dark clouds. Weather is the daily, short-term activity in the **atmosphere**. Unlike weather, **climate** does not change from day to day. Rather, climate is the **average** weather conditions over a

Vo•cab•u•lar•y

atmosphere (at•muh•sfeer)— all the air around us

climate (kly•mit)—the usual weather that occurs in a place, including the average temperature and average amounts of rain or wind

average (av•uhr•ij)—typical or usual level

[207]

Some climates on Earth are cold and wet—some are warm and wet.

very long period of time. We could say, for example, that Arizona has a warm, dry climate. On any one day, though, it might be cool. It might even rain. Because of its climate, Arizona is much more likely to be warm and dry than cool and wet.

There are many different climate regions on the earth. Some are warm and dry. Some are warm and wet. Still others are cold and wet. Does the earth itself have a climate? It does, and over its history, it has changed. Seventy million years ago, when the dinosaurs roamed, it was warmer than it is today just about everywhere on the earth. But about 12,000 years ago, during the last Ice Age, it was much cooler. Sheets of ice 2 miles thick covered parts of North America and Europe. The ice was thick enough to hide the Rocky Mountains beneath it. Some scientists believe that the earth's climate is in the process of changing again.

Hot Times Ahead?

Climate change is natural. But many people believe the earth's climate may be changing now partly because of the activity of human beings. Scientists are concerned about global warming—a heating up of the entire earth. Why are they concerned?

For one thing, the earth seems to be warming more quickly than at any time in the past. Since about 1890, the planet's temperature has risen about 1 degree Fahrenheit (a little more than half a degree Celsius). Some scientists predict it will go up 3°F in the next 50 years.

A change of 3 degrees may not seem like much.

Much of the southwestern United States is usually hot and dry.

But consider this: During the last Ice Age, the earth's average temperature was only 6°F lower than today. Knowing that, scientists fear a major impact on the way we live.

Clues in the Air

To understand why the earth is getting hotter, you need to understand why it is warm in the first place. Earth's atmosphere—the air we breathe—is a mixture of gases. The most common gases are **nitrogen, oxygen,** and **argon**. Together, they make up 99.9 percent of the atmosphere.

The remaining 0.1 percent—or one part in 1,000—is made up of small amounts of other gases. These are called trace gases. They include **carbon dioxide**—also called CO_2—and **methane**. Both play an important role in the atmosphere. Even tiny changes in their amounts could have a large impact on the earth's climate.

Living in a Greenhouse

Have you ever gotten into a car that has been parked in the sun on a hot summer day? If the car's windows have been closed, you feel how hot it gets inside. Because the glass has trapped the sun's heat, it is hotter inside the car than outside the car. The same thing happens in greenhouses. Greenhouses are used to grow plants because their windows trap the sun's heat. They can keep the plants inside warm even on the coldest days.

The same thing happens when sunlight strikes Earth. The sunlight carries heat, called solar **radiation**. It warms everything it touches—plants, dirt, water, animals, and even people. But these things don't keep all that heat. They lose—or radiate—some of it. Most of it passes back out into outer space. But a lot of it is trapped by the CO_2 and methane in the atmosphere. Those gases act like the windows on a greenhouse—they stop the heat from escaping. This process is known as the "greenhouse effect."

The greenhouse effect is a good and necessary thing. It makes life on the earth possible. Without it, Earth would be about 60°F colder than it is now. Most of our lakes, rivers, and even much of the ocean would freeze solid. Most plants would die, and so would most animals.

Vo·cab·u·lar·y

nitrogen (ny·truh·juhn)— a colorless, odorless gas that makes up about four fifths of the atmosphere. All plants and animals need nitrogen.

oxygen (ok·si·juhn)— a colorless, odorless, tasteless gas. It is needed for animals and plants to live.

argon (ar·gon)—a colorless, odorless gas that makes up about one percent of the earth's atmosphere

carbon dioxide (kar·buhn dy·ok·syd)— a colorless, odorless gas that is composed of carbon and oxygen and does not burn. It is produced when animals breathe and when fuel containing carbon burns.

methane (meth·ayn)— a colorless and odorless gas that burns easily; used as fuel

radiation (ray·dee·ay·shuhn)—the process of giving off energy in rays or waves

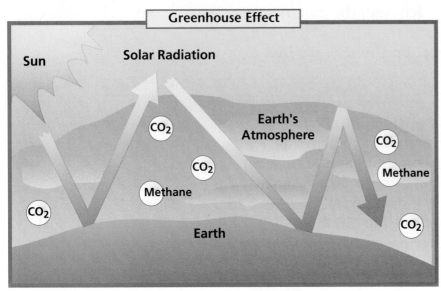

Greenhouse Effect

Sun

Solar Radiation

Earth's Atmosphere

CO_2 CO_2 CO_2 Methane Methane CO_2 CO_2

Earth

The sun's heat gets trapped in Earth's atmosphere.

There are places on the earth that are so cold that few things can live. Likewise, there are places so hot that not many plants or animals can survive. But most life exists in the middle of these two extremes. They live in places where the temperature is closer to the earth's average.

Meteorologists have been recording the weather since 1873. They know that the earth's average temperature has been rising over the past 100 years. During the 1980s and 1990s, average temperatures were the warmest they have been since the 1860s. The earth is getting warmer. Many scientists believe this is because the greenhouse gases in the atmosphere are increasing. In other words, the "windows" of "greenhouse Earth" are getting thicker. Why do these scientists think this?

Meteorologists can compare samples of the air today with samples from long ago. They get ancient air samples by drilling deeply into the ice caps at the North and South Poles.

The ice at the earth's poles is thousands of feet thick and full of air bubbles. Those bubbles hold air that has

A meteorologist checks his data.

Vo·**cab**·u·lar·y

meteorologists
(mee•tee•uh•**rol**•uh•jists)—
scientists who study the
atmosphere

been trapped there for tens of thousands of years. The farther down scientists drill into the ice caps, the older the air trapped there. These core samples show that the earth's CO_2 levels are rising faster now than they have in thousands of years. Why is this happening?

Meteorologists drill an ice cap to study ancient air.

Planes, Trains, Automobiles...and Cows?

Much of our modern society runs on what is called fossil fuels—coal, oil, and natural gas. We burn fossil fuels to run most of our machines. For example, power plants use fossil fuels to produce electricity. Millions and millions of cars and trucks use a fossil fuel—gasoline—to run. Gasoline is made from oil. When oil is burned, it releases CO_2 and other gases into the atmosphere. The more cars, trucks, and other machines people use, the more CO_2 is released. But this isn't the whole story about rising CO_2 levels.

Increased levels of CO_2 are also the result of destroying forest land. Trees **absorb** CO_2 from the air and use it to produce food for themselves. When there are fewer trees to absorb the gas, it stays in the atmosphere. If forest land is destroyed by burning, large amounts of carbon dioxide from the trees escape into the atmosphere.

Natural gas—another fossil fuel—is a mix of several gases. But natural gas is mostly methane. Like oil, it is used to heat people's homes. It is also used as a fuel for cooking. If it isn't burned when it is piped out of the ground, it escapes into the atmosphere.

Cows produce large quantities of methane gas.

There is another major source of rising methane levels. But it doesn't have anything to do with modern machinery. It is cows! As cows digest the grass they eat, they produce methane in their stomachs. There are now more than one billion cows on the earth! And each cow is releasing gas into the atmosphere!

It is clear that there is more CO_2 and more methane in our atmosphere today than in the past. It is also clear that these gases are making the earth warmer.

However, one very important question remains. What is still unclear is whether global warming is a bad thing.

Vo·cab·u·lar·y

absorb (uhb•sorb)—to take in and become part of

The Effects of Global Warming

So far, scientists can make only educated guesses about global warming. They use **equations** and computers. They study the oceans and clouds. And they apply what they learn to what they already know. For example, they know that Venus has so much CO_2 that the temperature on its surface is about 860°F! Even so, a few scientists believe that global warming—in moderation—might be good for the world. It might increase rainfall, for example. If so, land that is now too dry for growing food could become **fertile**. The huge Sahara Desert in Africa might again support farming—as it once did thousands of years ago.

However, global warming could be very bad. For one thing, warmer temperatures could cause the polar ice caps to melt. The melting ice would raise sea levels. Just a small rise would flood most of the world's coastal cities. Boston, Miami, and New Orleans might end up under water—as would New York and San Francisco. London, Tokyo, Venice, and Rio de Janeiro would be flooded, too.

Global warming would probably have a negative effect on wildlife as well. There are signs of trouble already. In North America and Europe, birds are migrating north earlier in the spring than they usually do. And plants are blooming earlier. Many insects depend on blooming plants for food. The insects, in turn, are eaten by many birds and animals. If the birds arrive before the insects hatch, the birds could starve. If the flowers bloom before the insects hatch, the insects could starve—and the flowers might not be able to pollinate.

What Can We Do?

The most obvious solution to prevent global warming is reducing our use of fossil fuels. This is an easy answer, but a difficult and expensive thing to do. All over the world, people depend on fossil fuels for heat, transportation, and to run machines. Most **economies** today are based on fossil fuels. This is especially true in the United States. Americans use one third of the earth's fossil fuels. And we have only one twentieth of the earth's population! But global warming is not just an American problem.

Vo•cab•u•lar•y

equations (i•**kway**•zhunz)— mathematical statements to show that two things are equal

fertile (**fur**•tl)—able to produce crops; rich

economies (i•**kon**•uh•meez) —the managing of money and materials

Global warming affects migrating birds.

In 2009, more than 190 countries met to discuss global warming. Many steps have been taken to correct the problem. One goal is finding sources of energy that do not pollute the air. Until those sources are found, there are some things we can do. But you have already taken the first step in solving the global warming problem. You are becoming **informed** about the problem.

Summary

The polar ice caps could melt. The oceans could rise. New York and San Francisco could be flooded by ocean waters. Rain might fall on the Sahara Desert and turn it into a fertile garden. Crops could grow where they've never grown before.

All of these things, some of them—or none of them—could occur through a process called global warming. Many scientists believe that Earth is getting warmer as a result of the greenhouse effect. Levels of carbon dioxide and methane—heat-trapping gases—are rising. Today most of these gases come from the burning of fossil fuels. Most scientists agree that global warming is a bad thing. The best way to prevent global warming is to find sources of energy other than fossil fuels.

Vo•**cab**•u•lar•y

informed—aware; knowledgeable

Root Words

Many words and word parts come from Latin and Greek. The word *sphere* comes from the Greek word *sphaira* and the Latin word *sphaera*, meaning "ball." *Sphere* is also the **root** of several words. The word *atmosphere* appears in "Global Warming: Too Much of a Good Thing?"

> *Weather is the daily, short-term activity in the **atmosphere**.*

The word *atmosphere* can be divided into a prefix and a root.

Prefix	+	Root
atmos- ("vapor")	+	*sphaera* ("ball")

The prefix and root suggest that *atmosphere* is the gases (vapors) that surround Earth (sphere).

People who study the atmosphere are called meteorologists. They study things in the atmosphere that affect the weather.

Match the scientist on the left to the "sphere"—or thing the scientist studies—on the right. Write your answers on a separate sheet of paper. Use a dictionary if you need help.

1. geographer　　　**a. hydrosphere** from the Greek word **hydor,** meaning "water"

2. glaciologist　　　**b. biosphere** from the Greek word **bios,** meaning "life"

3. astronomer　　　**c. lithosphere** from the Greek word **lithos,** meaning "stone"

4. biologist　　　**d. cryosphere** from the Greek word **kryos,** meaning "freezing"

5. oceanographer　　　**e. photosphere** from the Greek word **photos,** meaning "light or radiant energy"

Readers' Theater

The following script is a dialogue between a father and a son. Practice reading this script until you have a smooth, conversational tone.

Fluency **TIP**

Be sure to express the son's enthusiasm for his efforts and his excitement about teaching something to his father. For the father's part, be sure to express his interest in learning about what his son is saying and his respect for his son's dedication.

Dad Learns a Lesson About Recycling

Dad: Hey, Josh. That was a great game. Now I'm starving. Why don't we stop and get some food on the way home? How about some shakes and fries?

Josh: Well…I would like to celebrate, too. And I am hungry. But I can't do it, Dad. Not that way.

Dad: What do you mean, you can't do it THAT way?

Josh: In science class we're talking about recycling. Many of the fast-food places package everything in nonrecyclable materials. Our class went to four fast-food places. We bought something at each place. When we got back to class, we opened everything. Then we made a stack of the wrappers and cups and boxes from each place. You should have seen the size of our stacks!

Dad: OK, son. I think I'm getting the idea. But how's recycling going to help reduce global warming?

Josh: Recycling saves the trees. And saving trees reduces global warming. Trees absorb the gases in our air. If there are fewer trees, then that means the gases stay in the air. Those gases make Earth warmer.

Dad: I think I'm starting to get it now. Trees must be cut down to make paper products, such as food wrappers. As we cut down trees, we lose a way to absorb heat. Everything warms up more.

Josh: So if we use more recyclable products, we save more trees. And that is good for lots of reasons.

Dad: OK…I understand. But does that mean we are boycotting all fast-food restaurants?

Josh: Well, only the ones that are the worst at recycling.

Dad: I guess we have some research to do before we eat.

Josh: It will be worth it, Dad.

Map

Where the Asteroid Hit

You have been reading about an asteroid that might have caused the extinction of the dinosaurs. Some scientists believe they have found the crater that may have caused the extinction. The crater is in the Yucatán Peninsula on the Gulf of Mexico. The crater is 110 to 180 miles across. It is buried under 1,000 to 3,000 feet of limestone.

The map on the left shows Mexico and Central America. Look for the Gulf of Mexico and the Yucatán Peninsula. The map on the right shows a close-up of the area where the asteroid hit.

Study both maps and then answer the questions on the next page.

Discussion Questions

Answer these questions with a partner or on a separate sheet of paper.

1. Which statement is true about these two maps?
   a. The map on the right includes all the areas shown in the map on the left.
   b. The map on the left includes all the areas shown in the map on the right.
   c. Each map shows a different area.
   d. Both maps show exactly the same area.

2. Where did the asteroid probably kill some dinosaurs directly?
   a. United States
   b. Honduras
   c. Mexico
   d. Nicaragua

3. Do you think people who lived as far away as Costa Rica and Panama were harmed by the impact of the asteroid? Why or why not?

4. Which islands were closest to the impact?

5. Where do you live in relation to this crater?
   a. north
   b. northwest
   c. northeast
   d. south

6. Let's say that an asteroid did cause the extinction of the dinosaurs. Which of these happened first?
   a. An asteroid hit the Yucatán Peninsula.
   b. The Spaniards settled Mexico.
   c. The Panama Canal was created.
   d. The dinosaurs disappeared.

7. How might history have changed if the asteroid had landed in the middle of the Gulf of Mexico?

8. Is researching the reasons for the extinction of the dinosaurs a good use of scientists' time? Explain your answer.

EXPLORE MORE

Create a Chart

Work with a partner to create a chart showing the various theories explaining the disappearance of the dinosaurs. Draw pictures to illustrate the different ideas. Ask the class to vote on the theory they think is correct.

Write a Report

Research and write a report on one of the following topics from "Continents Adrift": volcanoes, convection, tectonic plates, or earthquakes. Be sure to include graphic aids to support your findings.

Hold a Press Conference

Research the findings of Sue, the most complete Tyrannosaurus rex skeleton ever found. Write a press release announcing the discovery of Sue to the media. Be prepared to answer questions!

Diagram a Volcano

Create a diagram of an active volcano. Label the different elements found in an active volcano. Explain what causes volcanoes to erupt. Diagram the different types of rock formations.

Write and Design a Brochure

Write and design a brochure on how to reduce our use of fossil fuels. Include findings on alternative sources of energy. Present evidence to support your findings. Be sure to include graphic aids.

Conduct a Debate

Work with a small group to hold a debate on global warming. One side should take the stand that global warming is a positive phenomenon, while the other side should argue that it may have a devastating effect on life on Earth.

Related Books

Day, Trevor. *Guide to Savage Earth.* Dorling Kindersley Limited, 2001.

Drake, Jane, and Ann Love. *Forestry.* Kids Can Press, 1998.

Friedman, Katherine. *What If the Polar Ice Caps Melted?* Children's Press, 2002.

Gallant, Roy A. *Dance of the Continents.* Benchmark Books, 2000.

—*Plates: Restless Earth.* Benchmark Books, 2003.

George, Linda. *Plate Tectonics.* Kidhaven Press, 2003.

Hawkes, Nigel. *Climate Crisis.* Copper Beech Books, 2000.

Hecht, Jeff. *Vanishing Life: The Mystery of Mass Extinctions.* Charles Scribner's Sons, 1993.

Johnson, Rebecca L. *The Greenhouse Effect: Life on a Warmer Planet.* Lerner Publications, 1993.

Kowalski, Kathiann M. *The Everything Kid's Nature Book.* Adams Media Corporation, 2000.

Matthews, Rupert. *End of the Dinosaurs.* Blackbirch Press, 2002.

Maze, Stephanie. *I Want to Be...An Environmentalist.* Harcourt, Inc., 2000.

Nardo, Don. *The Extinction of the Dinosaurs.* Lucent Books, 2002.

Oxlade, Chris. *Global Warming.* Bridgestone Books, 2003.

Pringle, Laurence P. *Global Warming: The Threat of Earth's Changing Climate.* SeaStar Books, 2001.

Relf, Pat. *The Story of the Colossal Fossil.* Scholastic, Inc., 2000.

Sattler, Helen Roney. *Our Patchwork Planet: The Story of Plate Tectonics.* Lothrop, Lee and Shepard, 1995.

Shaw, Jane S. *Global Warming.* Greenhaven Press, 2002.

Stein, Paul. *Storms of the Future.* Rosen Publishing Group, 2001.

Taylor, Barbara. *How to Save the Planet.* Franklin Watts, 2001.

Weidner, Zoehfeld. *Dinosaur Parents, Dinosaur Young: Uncovering the Mystery of Dinosaur Families.* Clarion Books, 2001.

Weller, Dave, and Mick Hart. *Arctic and Antarctic.* Thunder Bay Press, 1996.

Interesting Web Sites

Dinosaurs
http://paleobiology.si.edu/dinosaurs
http://www.dinosaurfact.net

Continents
http://pubs.usgs.gov/gip/dynamic/dynamic.html

Global Warming
http://www.exploratorium.edu/climate/
http://www.epa.gov/climatechange/kids/

Web sites have been carefully researched for accuracy, content, and appropriateness. However, teachers and caregivers are reminded that Web sites are subject to change. Internet use should always be monitored.

BEFORE READING

Set a Purpose

by skimming the selection to decide what I want to know about this subject.

DURING READING

Clarify Understanding

by deciding whether the information I'm reading is fact or opinion.

AFTER READING

Respond

by forming my own opinion about what I've read.

LEARN
the strategies
in the selection
A Real Television Hero
page 223

PRACTICE
the *strategies*
in the selection
Pioneering a New Language
page 237

APPLY
the *strategies*
in the selection
Weaving the World Together
page 249

Think About the
Strategies

BEFORE READING

Set a Purpose

by skimming the selection to decide what I want to know about this subject.

> **My Thinking**
>
> This strategy says to set a purpose for reading by skimming the selection to decide what I want to know about. I see pictures of a car, a plow, and television sets. I want to know how these things are all connected. From the heading "Drawn by Electricity," I think I'm going to learn how these things might work. I would like to learn who invented them and how.

DURING READING

Clarify Understanding

by deciding whether the information I'm reading is fact or opinion.

> **My Thinking**
>
> This strategy says to decide whether the information I'm reading is fact or opinion. I will stop and think about this strategy every time I come to a red button like this ⊙.

A Real Television Hero

Philo Farnsworth with an early model of his invention

Philo Farnsworth changed your life, but you have probably never heard of him. He was born in a log cabin in Utah in 1906. However, Philo did not live there long. He and his family moved many times. They lived in small towns and on farms. They finally settled on his uncle's ranch in Idaho. The family made several moves in wagons pulled by horses. Some people had cars back then, but Philo's family could not afford one. But that changed.

By the time Philo died in 1971, he had his own car. He also held 300 **patents** on his inventions. Philo was a pioneer in the development of television.

Vo·cab·u·lar·y

patents (pat•nts)—papers giving only the holder of the invention the right to make, use, or sell it

Drawn by Electricity

Philo's fascination with electricity began the first time he saw electric toy trains and electric motors in a Sears catalogue. Yet his family did not have electricity until they moved to his uncle's ranch in 1919. At that time, Philo was 13. Philo's family had hoped he would someday become a concert violinist, but Philo had other plans. He was drawn to electricity.

Philo quickly found the **generator** that produced electricity for the ranch. From then on, Philo spent all his spare time experimenting with it. He often caused it to stop working. Some weeks, his mother had to call for repairs two or three times to get the generator fixed.

During these repair visits, Philo paid close attention to how the repairs were made. Soon, he was able to repair it himself. Then he started connecting other machines to the generator. Once he figured everything out, he hooked up his mother's washing machine to the generator. Next, Philo hooked up his mother's sewing machine. Soon the generator did all of the work! Then he added electric lights to his uncle's barn. Young Philo was soon asked to wire other buildings in town for electricity.

To learn more about electricity, Philo read all the science magazines he could find. Although most people did not yet have radios, Philo read about an idea for **transmitting** pictures, called television. Now that was exciting—a machine that could receive pictures! He decided to see if he could make a television.

Vo•cab•u•lar•y

generator (jen•uh•ray•tuhr)— a machine that changes the energy of movement into useful electricity

transmitting (trans•mit•ing) —sending from one place to another by radio waves or wire

Philo discovered he could make household appliances work on electricity when he connected them to a generator.

While Philo was experimenting with his ideas, he entered a contest. The Ford Motor Company was offering $25 for an invention to improve the automobile. That was a lot of money back then. Philo's family still did not have a car. Philo had an idea for a way to start a car without **cranking** it. He invented an **ignition** that would start the car only if a special key was used. The key had to be **magnetized** by electricity. He had used what he knew about electricity to win the prize. Thieves would no longer be able to steal cars with a simple turn of the crank.

The Ford Model T

The Picture Becomes Clearer

In 1920, when Philo was in the ninth grade, he was allowed to take a twelfth grade science class. His teacher was amazed at Philo's questions. Philo was not just curious. He was looking for ways to send pictures over wires.

One day, Philo was **plowing** a field at his uncle's ranch. He noticed the pattern of straight lines he was making in the soil. He wondered what would happen if he divided a picture into small pieces, the way the lines were dividing the field. Then he could change each piece of the picture into a bit of electricity and send it through a wire. When the bits of electricity reached the television set, they could be changed back into pieces of the picture.

Vo·cab·u·lar·y

cranking (**krangk**•ing)— starting a car by turning on the engine with a crank in the front

ignition (ig•**nish**•uhn)— the part of a car that makes it start

magnetized (**mag**•ni•tyzd) —able to attract metals; many metals are magnetized when electricity passes through them

plowing—breaking up soil in rows for planting

Straight lines in the soil (above) gave Philo an idea. He could divide a picture into straight lines. Straight lines (inset) make up the picture on a television screen.

Philo was really excited about his idea. With his science teacher's help, he learned about special glass tubes called cathode-ray tubes (CRT). All the air is removed from these tubes. Because of this and what he knew about electricity, he was sure that his pieces of pictures would be able to move more easily.

At the age of 14, Philo used a cathode-ray tube in his design for an electronic television. It was made of a television camera and a television receiver. In the camera, the picture would be divided up and changed into a pattern of electricity. In the receiver (the cathode-ray tube), the pattern of electricity would be changed back into a picture.

Using Text Features

Diagram Review the diagram of a cathode-ray tube. What is the process it shows?

Answer: The diagram shows that electrons flow through the cathode-ray tube and strike the phosphor coating. As they strike the phosphor coating, the electrons glow, producing light on the screen.

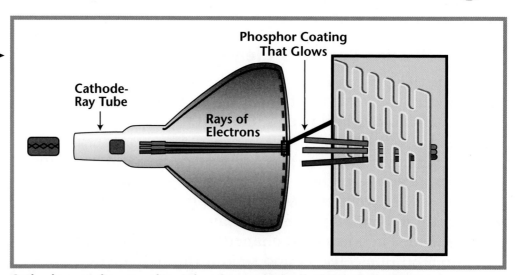

Cathode-ray tubes are glass tubes from which all of the air has been removed. They are coated with a glowing substance that produces light at a certain point on a screen when electricity flows through the tubes.

A Bumpy Road to Success

When he was 15, Philo started college at Brigham Young University in Utah. However, he did not stay long. His father had passed away, and he was needed to support his family. Also, Philo still had many ideas that he wanted to try out. Soon, he was able to produce his first receiver. It measured only 4 inches across. The picture was black and white.

In 1927, at the age of 21, Philo applied for a patent for his television invention so no one else could use his idea. In 1934, a British company bought a license from Philo so it could use his design. In 1939, the Radio Corporation of America (RCA) also bought a license from Philo. Then the British company and RCA competed with each other and with Philo to make the first television sets for the public. Unfortunately, Philo did not have enough money or staff to keep up with these huge companies. The companies made the money from Philo's invention, but Philo remained proud that a huge company like RCA had to pay him licensing fees.

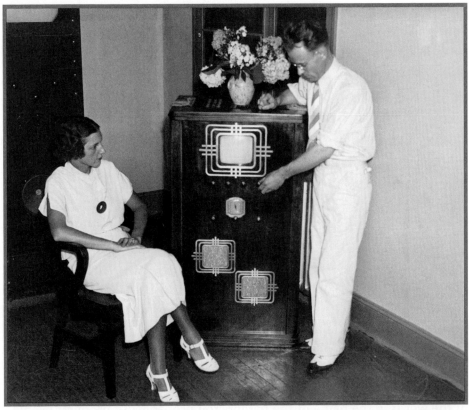

Philo demonstrating his invention

By the end of World War II in 1945, television was no longer a strange idea. Television shows were being **broadcast** daily. Television sets were beginning to appear in people's homes. Philo spent his time working on ways to improve his original idea. For example, he discovered a way to make a cathode-ray tube that would not heat up.

Philo's Patents

Television System

Television Receiving System

Television Scanning and Synchronizing System

Electron Image Amplifier

System of Pulse Transmission

Thermionic Vacuum Tube

Luminescent Screen

Image Dissector

Projection Apparatus

Cathode-Ray Tube

Image Analysis

X-Ray Projection Device

Electric Recording and Reproducing System

Television Projection System

Color Television Apparatus

Radio Translating Device

Light Translating Device

Method and Apparatus for Producing Nuclear Fusion Reactions

Microwave Amplifier

This chart lists just some of Philo T. Farnsworth's hundreds of patents. Do you recognize some of these devices? If not, you probably recognize some of the words in the name of the patent. You probably use products every day that were developed as a result of Philo's patents.

Vo·cab·u·lar·y

broadcast (**brawd**•kast)— sent out by means of television or radio signals

18th, 19th, and 20th Century Inventions

1752 Benjamin Franklin's Lightning Rod
1794 Eli Whitney's Cotton Gin
1806 Coffeepot
1807 Steamboat
1833 Sewing Machine
1844 Telegraph
1845 False Teeth
1857 Passenger Elevator
1863 Roller Skates
1873 Typewriter
1876 Telephone
1884 Thrill Ride (Roller Coaster named Switchback)
1885 Skyscraper (10-story building in Chicago)
1888 Kodak Camera
1889 Dishwasher
1891 Escalator
1893 Zipper
1902 Air Conditioning
1903 Airplane
1908 Model T Ford Automobile
1927 Philo T. Farnsworth's Television
1929 Frozen Food
1931 Radio Astronomy
1940 Jeep
1947 Polaroid Camera
1948 Electric Guitar
1955 Nuclear Submarine
1972 Video Game
1976 Super Computer
1982 Artificial Heart
1983 Personal Computer
1990 Hubble Telescope
1990 World Wide Web
1993 GPS
1995 DVD
2001 iPod
2003 Hybrid Automobile
2005 YouTube

More Than Just the Inventor of Television

Philo did not see electricity in use until he was 13. However, he had already thought of many ways he could put it to work. His ideas led to 300 patents, mostly in the field of radio and television. However, he invented many other things, too. He was responsible for some of the inventions used during World War II. For example, he invented the process of using radio waves to get direction. Do you know what it is called now? Radar. He also invented the black light used for seeing at night. He is responsible for the Defense Early Warning Signal, the infrared telescope, submarine detection devices, the PPI Projector used for ground control of air traffic, and the infant incubator. He also contributed something to medicine—an electronic microscope. He even did research on peaceful uses of **atomic energy**. Before he died in 1971, Philo had been working on a nuclear fusion process to produce clean, virtually unlimited energy. In fact, he would probably be proud to know that his work with cold nuclear fusion is progressing at the University of Utah. It is also earning international attention.

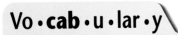
Vo·cab·u·lar·y

atomic energy (uh•**tom**•ik **en**•uhr•jee)—energy made when the tiniest parts of matter split or join

Apollo 11 astronaut Edwin "Buzz" Aldrin walks on the moon.

Looking Back

In 1969, Philo Farnsworth watched as television showed the first astronauts walking on the moon. "This has made it all worthwhile," he told his wife. Philo had never dreamed of traveling to the moon. However, his ideas helped us see that first step on the moon and many other things. If Philo were alive today, he might be honored to know that he was one of four inventors issued a stamp bearing his likeness by the U.S. Postal Service in 1983. The next time you turn on your television, you can thank Philo.

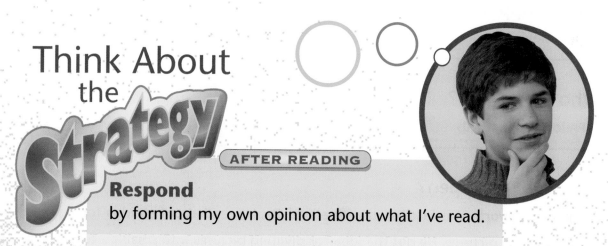

Think About the Strategy

AFTER READING

Respond

by forming my own opinion about what I've read.

My Thinking

The strategy says to respond to the selection by forming my own opinion about what I've read. I think that Philo Farnsworth was a great inventor. I'm glad he invented the television. He must have been very smart to research and invent so many things. I think it is too bad that he did not get the money for inventing the television. But I'm very glad he got to see the first man walk on the moon through his own invention—the television.

Graphic organizers help us organize information we read. I think this article can be organized by using a 5 Ws Chart. A 5 Ws Chart will help answer the following questions: What happened? Who was there? Why did it happen? When did it happen? Where did it happen? Here is how I answered these questions and organized the information.

5 Ws Chart
A Real Television Hero

What Happened?

The television was invented.

Who Was There?

Philo T. Farnsworth

Why Did It Happen?

Philo Farnsworth was fascinated with electricity. He read about an idea for transmitting pictures. He got the idea for dividing pictures into small pieces while plowing a field. Then he began experimenting.

When Did It Happen?

In 1927, Philo applied for a patent for the television. By 1945, television shows were being broadcast daily.

Where Did It Happen?

It all started on a ranch in Idaho.

I used my graphic organizer to write a summary of the article. Can you find the information in my summary that came from my 5 Ws Chart?

A Summary of
A Real Television Hero

Can you imagine an invention that would change everybody's lives? This invention would make young people happy and old people happy—plus everybody in between. You might wonder what you would ever do without it. You also might wonder what people did before it was invented!

A day without television seems like a strange idea now. Television is part of our lives. But years ago, television was a strange idea.

So who is responsible for inventing television? Who created this thing that changed everybody's lives forever? It was Philo Farnsworth.

When Philo was a little boy, he was fascinated by the electric trains and motors he saw in catalogues. As he grew older, he experimented with electricity. One day Philo was plowing a field on his uncle's ranch. He got an idea. The plow was dividing the field into small pieces. In a similar way, Philo could divide a picture into little bits of electricity. Next, the pieces could be sent over wires. Then they could be put back together. They would form the same picture.

Philo experimented with his idea. In 1927, when he was only 21, he applied for a patent for a television. By 1945, people were watching television in their very own homes. Soon millions of people had TVs.

From one ranch in Idaho and one young man's imagination came a great invention. Now televisions are found all over the world.

It's hard to imagine life without television. Television can teach us and entertain us. Thank you, Philo, for your imagination, talent, and courage.

Introduction
My introductory paragraph tells readers what they are about to read.

Body
Each of my body paragraphs has information from one of the 5W question rows. My first body paragraph tells exactly **what** the invention in this article is. My second body paragraph tells **who** invented it, and the third tells **why** it all happened. My fourth body paragraph explains **when** the invention took place, and my last body paragraph tells **where** it all happened.

Conclusion
I summarized my paper by telling a little about what television has done for people. I also thanked the inventor for all of his work!

Compound Words

A **compound word** is a word that is made by putting two smaller words together. The meanings of the two smaller words can help you find the meaning of the compound word.

The compound word in boldface below is from "A Real Television Hero."

> *Television shows were being* **broadcast** *daily.*
> When you take *broadcast* apart, you get two words.
> *broad* ("far and wide") + *cast* ("to throw or hurl")

Together the two words make the new word *broadcast,* which means "to transmit (throw) to a large (broad) area."

Other compound words found in the selection are:

> *steam* ("water vapor") + *boat* ("a craft for traveling on water") = *steamboat,* meaning "a boat that is driven by a steam engine"

> *dish* ("a container for holding food") + *washer* ("a machine for washing") = *dishwasher,* meaning "a machine that washes dishes"

Find the correct compound word in the list to complete each sentence below. Write your answers on a separate sheet of paper. Then write a definition for each word. Look your definitions up in a dictionary, if necessary.

castaway	broadsided	broadband
forecast	broadloom	

1. A truck almost _____ our car when we were on the highway.

2. I always check the weather _____ on the nightly news.

3. The _____ carpet covered the lovely wooden floor.

4. The poor _____ was stranded on the island for seven years.

5. He was a pioneer in the field of _____ communications.

Dialogue

Read aloud this short made-up conversation between young Philo Farnsworth and his tutor, Justin Tolman. The dialogue begins and ends with the voice of a narrator. Read it with two friends.

> **TIP** Experiment with different ways of using your voice to express excitement, curiosity, and maybe a little doubt.

A Chemistry Lesson?

Narrator: Justin Tolman, Philo's tutor, enters the room where Philo is working. He is ready to begin a tutoring session with Philo, but Philo is busy working on something else. What do you think it could be?

Justin Tolman: Philo, are you ready for your chemistry studies?

Philo: Just one minute. I want to show you something. Let me finish this last diagram on the chalkboard.

Justin Tolman: What are all these equations you've written? This chalkboard is full!

Philo: I have an idea.

Narrator: Justin walks over to the chalkboard and looks at what Philo is writing. He has a puzzled expression on his face.

Justin Tolman: These aren't chemical equations. What is this diagram? What does any of this have to do with chemistry?

Philo: Nothing, really. I've got this idea, and I have to tell you about it now. You're the only person I know who can understand it.

Narrator: Justin nods his head. He is very interested in what Philo is doing.

Justin Tolman: Yes, well, you certainly have my attention. I can hardly wait to hear your explanation for all of this.

Philo: I'm going to make an electronic television.

Justin Tolman: Electronic what? What is television?

Philo: Oh, you'll see.

Narrator: Yes, Justin will soon see—as will the whole world!

Think About the Strategies

BEFORE READING

Set a Purpose

by skimming the selection to decide what I want to know about this subject.

 Write notes on your own paper to tell how you used this strategy.

DURING READING

Clarify Understanding

by deciding whether the information I'm reading is fact or opinion.

 When you come to a red button like this 🔴, write notes on your own paper to tell how you used this strategy.

Pioneering a New Language

Augusta Ada Byron King, Countess of Lovelace, known as Ada, had a strange start for a pioneer. She was born into a wealthy London family in 1815. Ada was the child of the famous English poet Lord Byron. Her mother also came from a wealthy family. At that time, the only thing British society seemed to expect from wealthy girls and women was a pleasant smile and good manners. As a teenager, Ada spent much of her time attending plays, going to parties, and dancing at balls.

Yet Ada became one of the few women mathematicians of her time. She was the world's first computer **programmer,** male or female. In 1979, the U.S. Department of Defense named its main computer language "Ada" after her.

Vo·**cab**·u·lar·y

programmer
(**proh**•gram•uhr)—a person who prepares programs, or the sets of instructions, for computers

A Poetic and Mathematical Beginning

Ada never knew her father, Lord Byron. He and Ada's mother didn't get along. They had very different interests. He was a poet and she loved math and science. Lord Byron even wrote a letter to his wife about math. Can you tell from this letter that he was more interested in poetry than he was in math?

I agree with you quite upon Mathematics
  too—and must be content
To admire them at a...distance—I know
  that two and two make four—
and should be glad to prove it too if
  I could—though I must say
if by any sort of process I
  could convert two and
  two into five
  it would give me much
  greater pleasure.

When Ada was only seven weeks old, she and her mother went to live with her mother's parents. Several weeks later, Lord Byron left England and never again saw his wife or daughter. Ada was raised by her mother and grandparents. Lord Byron died in Greece when Ada was eight years old.

Lord Byron

Education Before Social Graces

During the early 1800s, the daughters of wealthy British families were required to learn the "social graces." They needed to prepare for all the parties they would attend. These young women studied music, painting, and languages. Ada, however, preferred museums and **lectures** to parties. She was a member of the Bluestockings, a women's social and educational society. The emphasis, however, was placed on education over socializing. Ada's mother had always encouraged education. She wanted her daughter to study math and science. Ada agreed and enjoyed her studies. Math seemed to come easily to her. When she was only 5 years old, she was able to add 6 rows of numbers. Before she turned 13, she was studying **geometry**. Ada was taught at home by private tutors. Later, she studied on her own.

One of Ada's tutors was Augustus de Morgan. He made some important mathematical discoveries. But he had some poetic interests, too. He is known for modifying a poem written by the English author Jonathan Swift. Can you find the mathematical references in the poem?

Great fleas have little fleas upon their backs to bite 'em,
And little fleas have lesser fleas, and so ad infinitum.
And the great fleas themselves, in turn, have greater fleas
While these again have greater still, and greater still, and
so on.

A Chance Meeting

At one of many parties, Ada happened to meet Charles Babbage. He was a scientist, mathematician, and inventor. One of his inventions was the **speedometer,** a device that tells drivers how fast they are going. He also invented the skeleton key, which is a key that can open any door. Babbage invented the **ophthalmoscope,** too, an instrument that allows doctors to look at the back of the eye. In addition, he created a machine that could solve math problems and print the answers. He called this invention the analytical engine. Ada visited his home and saw a model of the machine. She immediately understood how it worked. Babbage and Ada decided to work together.

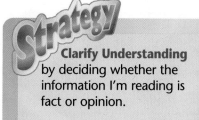

Strategy

Clarify Understanding by deciding whether the information I'm reading is fact or opinion.

Write notes on your own paper to tell how you used this strategy.

Vo•cab•u•lar•y

lectures (lek•chuhrz)— informative talks on serious topics

geometry (jee•om•i•tree)— the part of mathematics that deals with the measurement and relationships of points, lines, and angles in surfaces and solids

speedometer (spi•dom•i•tuhr)—a device that measures and indicates speed, as of an automobile

ophthalmoscope (of•thal•muh•skohp)— an instrument used for studying the inside structure of the eye

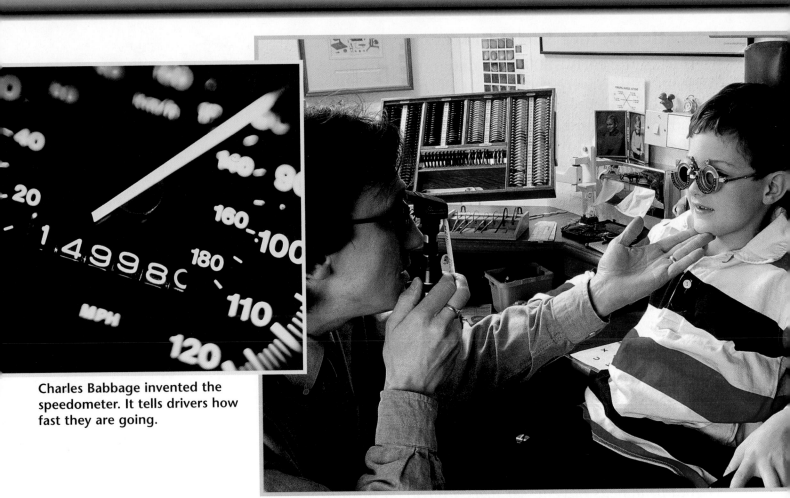

Charles Babbage invented the speedometer. It tells drivers how fast they are going.

A doctor tests a young patient's eyes using an ophthalmoscope.

Too Far Ahead of Its Time?

At first, the British government gave Babbage money to build his analytical engine. Then the government changed its mind and decided not to support the project. He didn't mind. He already had an idea for a new invention, which would become the first computer. It would be able to read and store information, solve math problems, carry out the user's instructions, and print the answers.

Charles Babbage's invention was never built, partly because it was too far ahead of its time. The technology in the mid-1800s was not advanced enough to turn his ideas into a working machine. Also, the British government was not interested in paying for any more of his projects. Nevertheless, Ada wrote sets of instructions for solving math problems using this machine. Today we would call this computer programming. Ada wrote programs for Babbage's machine even though it was never built.

Charles Babbage

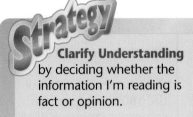
Clarify Understanding by deciding whether the information I'm reading is fact or opinion.

 Write notes on your own paper to tell how you used this strategy.

The Countess of Lovelace

In her early twenties, Ada continued her work with Charles Babbage. However, her personal life took a different turn. She met William King, also known as Lord Lovelace. He was proud of her achievements and encouraged her work. In those days, most women did not work in math or science. Ada married Lord Lovelace. After Ada married Lord Lovelace, she decided to sign her work "A.A.L." instead of using her name. Few people knew that those were the initials of Augusta Ada Byron King, Countess of Lovelace.

Over the years, Ada continued to work with Charles Babbage off and on. However, she was greatly bothered by his careless work habits and lack of organization. At one point, she asked him to sign an agreement to change his ways. He refused. But they did work together on other projects.

In her thirties, Ada became sick with cancer. She died of the disease in 1852. She was only 36 years old. That is the same age at which her father died.

Using
Text Features

Chart Review the chart to see how words used for the analytical engine of the 1800s compare with computer language used today. Then work with a partner to create a chart that compares another category of words from two different time periods. Share your chart with the class.

Words From Yesterday and Today

The following chart compares words used for the analytical engine with contemporary computer language.

Yesterday	Today
accidental sign	sign bit
analyst	programmer
attendant	operator
column (or rack)	memory (RAM) cell
cycle	loop
rack (of columns)	Random Access Memory (RAM)
stepping down	right shift
stepping up	left shift
turn of the handle	clock cycle

Ada's Legacy

Imagine what Ada might say if she were alive today and could walk through a manufacturing plant, a laboratory, a mall, an office, or even a home. She would probably be amazed at how computers have influenced our lives. She might also be pleased at the way the U.S. Department of Defense honored her contributions to computer technology. Ada did not write the programming language that the Department of Defense named after her, but her work helped make modern computer programming possible.

Ada also had a vision of the future. She believed that someday computer machines would be able to create graphics and compose music. Do you think Ada would be proud to know that her predictions have come true?

Ada did have some idea of how her work might be used someday. However, she warned against depending too much on computers. She wrote that they can do only what we program them to do. They do not think for themselves, so we must be careful!

More than 150 years after Ada's death, we have a shorter way to say this: "Garbage in, garbage out." Computer programmers and users still have to do a lot of thinking. If they put in errors, they get errors back.

What Is Your Computer I.Q.?

See how many of the computer equipment names you know. Write the answers on your own piece of paper. (The answers are upside-down below this chart—no peeking!)

Computer Equipment and Data

#		
①		Output
②		Input
③		Input
④		Output
⑤		Long-term storage
⑥		Long-term storage

Can You Program a Computer?

Many students use computers in schools today. Some are even learning to program computers. At a beginning level, these students can use drawing programs to create scenes. Later, students can add movement to their scenes. Ada would probably be pleased that young students, both boys and girls, are not only using computers but also learning to program them.

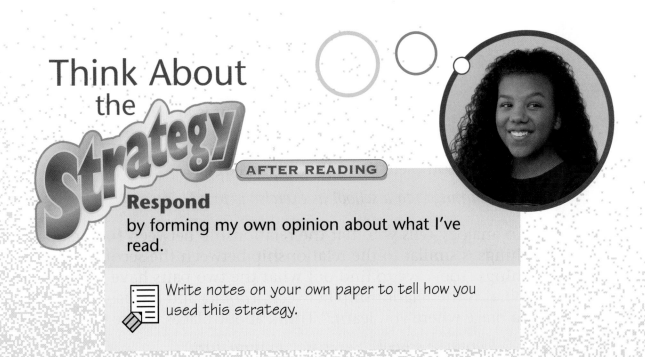

Think About the Strategy

AFTER READING

Respond
by forming my own opinion about what I've read.

Write notes on your own paper to tell how you used this strategy.

Developing Vocabulary

Analogies

An **analogy** is a kind of comparison. It tells how things are alike. Analogies are used in tests to check your understanding of vocabulary.

Here is a part of the chart from "Pioneering a New Language."

Yesterday	Today
analyst	programmer
attendant	operator

The author is comparing names used in the past with names used today. If the above words were written as an analogy, it would probably look like this:

Analyst is to programmer as attendant is to operator.
or *analyst : programmer : : attendant : operator*

Can you complete the following analogy?

Learning is to a school as exercise is to a _____.

An analogy tells you that the relationship between the first pair of things is similar to the relationship between the second pair of things. You have to find out what the two pairs have in common. What is the relationship between *learning* and a *school*? A *school* is "a place where you learn." Think about places where you *exercise*.

*learning : school : : exercise : **gymnasium***

Use the following words to complete each analogy. Write your answers on a separate sheet of paper.

geometry   monitor   keyboard   speedometer   document

1. file : _____ : : book : page
2. thermometer : temperature : : _____ : speed
3. _____ : type : : mouse : click
4. geology : rocks : : _____ : angles
5. _____ : picture : : speaker : sound

Limericks

Limericks are funny five-line poems. The first, second, and fifth lines rhyme, as do the shorter third and fourth lines. Limericks originated in Limerick, Ireland. Practice reading the following limericks until your delivery is smooth and has a singsong feel to it.

Practice the limericks silently and orally. Then read them to your teacher or classmates. Ask them to tell you what you did well and what you might improve.

ROTFL

There once was a young girl named Nell
Who thought that all e-mail was swell.
A funny young bloke
Just e-mailed a joke.
And now Nell's ROTFL*.

* ROTFL = Rolling On The Floor Laughing

Young Ada

The sassy young daughter of Byron
Was a girl that we can't help admirin'.
There was no disputing
Her knack for computing.
Pure genius! Of that I'm not lyin'.

Fast Fingers

There was a young fellow from Brightning
Whose fingers could type fast as lightning.
He quite overloaded.
His keyboard exploded!
And the look on his face was quite frightening.

Think About
the
Strategies

Set a Purpose
by skimming the selection to decide what I want
to know about this subject.

Clarify Understanding
by deciding whether the information I'm reading
is fact or opinion.

Respond
by forming my own opinion about what I've
read.

 Use your own paper to jot notes to apply these
Before, During, and After Reading Strategies. In
this selection, you will choose when to stop,
think, and respond.

Weaving the World Together

How do you use the World Wide Web? Do you look for information for school reports? Do you do searches on topics that interest you? Do you e-mail your friends and family members? Do your parents sometimes shop **online**? Today, millions of people use the Web. It was invented by a man named Tim Berners-Lee. He proposed the idea of the World Wide Web in 1989. In 1991, computer users were first able to use the Web. Now it's an important part of modern life.

The Web or the Internet?

Do you know the difference between the Web and the Internet? They are not the same. The Internet is a network of networks made from computers and cables. The Web is

Vo·cab·u·lar·y

online—connected through a system, especially a computer system

Tim Berners-Lee

a way to send information over the Internet. The Web is made of **documents** and **files**.

The Internet provides the connections so the documents and files of the Web can be delivered where they are sent.

The Internet was designed in 1973 by a number of people. After ten years of improvements, it was made available for public use in 1983. The person responsible for inventing the system to send information over the Internet is Tim Berners-Lee. However, Tim stresses that his Web could not exist without the Internet. The Web depends on the connections provided by the Internet.

How the Web Was Woven

Tim was born in 1955 in London, England. His parents were both mathematicians. They met while they were helping to develop the first kind of computer to be sold in stores.

As a child, Tim loved knowing how electricity makes things work. When he entered The Queen's College at Oxford University, he studied physics. He believes that his background in **physics** has helped him think in clear, planned ways. Tim graduated in 1976. For the next several years, he worked for computer companies, designing **software** and computer systems.

By 1990, Tim was working for CERN, a physics laboratory in Switzerland. While there, he invented a new kind of notebook for himself. He used it to keep track of the people and projects he was working with and how they were connected. This pioneer of the computer age then used the idea behind his notebook to create a model of the Web. He designed the Web as a way to combine or link documents by using hypertext. A hypertext document contains links to other documents. If you click on a certain word or phrase in a hypertext document, a related document will appear on your computer screen. Often, the hypertext is printed in blue to make it easy to locate. Hypertext helps people work together by linking their knowledge in a web.

Vo•cab•u•lar•y

documents (**doc**•yuh•muhnts)—pieces of writing that convey information, whether electronically or on paper

files—groups of documents stored together, whether electronically or in paper file folders

physics (**fiz**•iks)—the study of matter and energy and how they interact

software (**sawft**•wair)—computer programs; the codes that tell a computer what to do

Tim works for the Massachusetts Institute of Technology (M.I.T.).

In August of 1991, Tim put his new Web on the Internet. It immediately attracted users and continues to do so. In 1994, Tim went to work for the Laboratory for Computer Science at the Massachusetts Institute of Technology. He is now in charge of the World Wide Web **Consortium** (W3C). This group is responsible for guiding the development of the Web. It helps the Web reach its potential. It sets standards for the Web, including the kinds of technology that can be used. It also settles disagreements related to the Web and its use. In this way, W3C helps keep the Web from breaking into many smaller webs. If it broke up, communication between webs would be complicated and difficult. It might not even be possible to move information from one web to another.

Vo•cab•u•lar•y

consortium
(kuhn•**sor**•tee•uhm)—a group that is formed to perform a task no one member could do alone

[251]

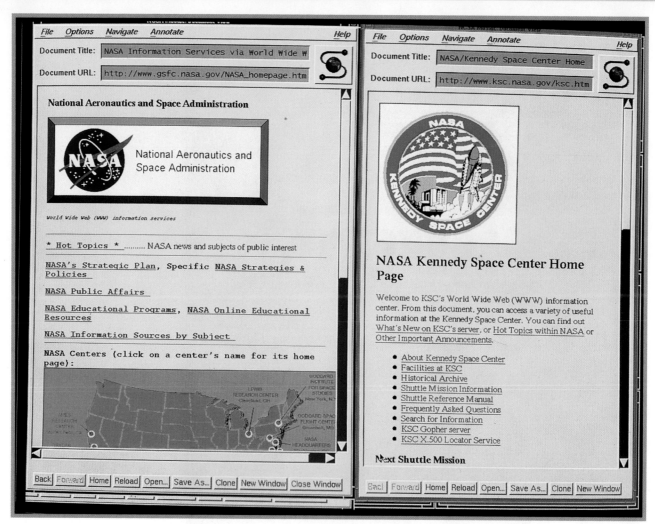

Sample home pages of NASA and the Kennedy Space Center

Praise for a Pioneer

As the Web continues to pull us all together, *Time* magazine has chosen Tim as one of the great minds of the twentieth century. *Time* says that the full effect of Tim's pioneering work will not be known for years. The list of Tim's awards is long and growing, as people begin to appreciate what he has done.

You might wonder whether Tim made millions of dollars from his idea for linking sites and helping people share their knowledge. The answer is "no." As soon as he entered the Web on the Internet, it belonged to everyone. He knew he could no longer control it or make money from it. Although the W3C tries to maintain certain standards, no one owns the World Wide Web.

Time Line

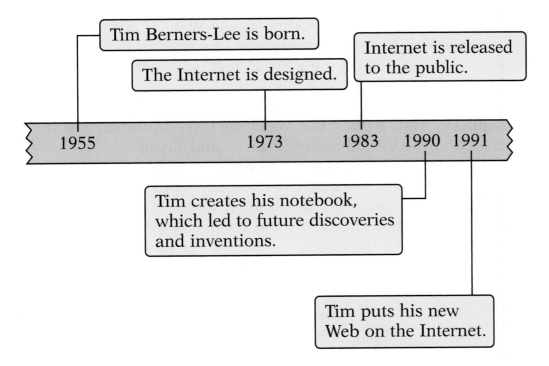

Tim Berners-Lee is born.

The Internet is designed.

Internet is released to the public.

| 1955 | 1973 | 1983 | 1990 | 1991 |

Tim creates his notebook, which led to future discoveries and inventions.

Tim puts his new Web on the Internet.

Because of this lack of control, Web sites are not checked for accuracy. Tim cautions Web users to watch out for biased or one-sided information. Some sites, for example, are personal Web pages. They may look **official,** but they offer only the owner's opinions. Tim urges Web users to think carefully about the information offered by all sites. You can't assume something is correct just because it is on the Web.

Still, he is pleased with the way his idea has taken shape and been developed. He believes that the Web allows people to communicate and work together in ways no one imagined in years past. This communication, Tim believes, may lead to many needed changes. It has already resulted in changes in the way we do business, the way we exchange ideas, and even the way we shop and entertain. Tim is satisfied that his contribution, the World Wide Web, will be a major influence on our lives from now on. That's payment enough for him.

Vo•cab•u•lar•y

official (uh•**fish**•uhl)—
coming from an authority

Do You Want to Help Manage the World Wide Web?

If you really enjoy using the World Wide Web, you may be interested in someday working for the W3C. It is a big responsibility, but you would always be right in the middle of what is happening on the Web. In fact, you might even be in charge of some aspects of the Web.

The W3C team is made up of talented researchers and engineers from around the world. Its three headquarters are located in the United States, France, and Japan.

Some of the subjects you will need to study to get ready for jobs like these are math, science, computer science and technology, and physics, just to name a few. In addition to technical abilities, the W3C looks for people who have insight, tact, and the ability to follow things through. Being able to work as part of a team is also very important.

These students are using the World Wide Web to help them in school. Maybe someday they, and you, will work for the W3C.

Being a member of the W3C is a big responsibility. Would you like to be a member someday? If so, take a look at the kinds of issues you will need to learn about. It's a big job! Are you ready?

World Wide Web Consortium
Facing the Challenges of Tomorrow

As with all technologies, the World Wide Web is always changing. The W3C wants to be prepared for the challenges the future may bring. What is the W3C doing to prepare for the future?

1. The W3C wants to make sure the World Wide Web can be used by everyone. They are working on ways for technology to keep up with how people use the Web. How do you or your parents or teachers access the World Wide Web: computer, cellular phone, TV, digital camera, in-car computer? What device do you, or they, use for access: keypad, mouse, voice? The W3C has a big responsibility to keep up with technology and the ways people use it.

2. The W3C wants to promote best practices. This means that they are responsible for writing guidelines about the best and the right ways to use the Web. They are also responsible for answering questions from the public about the use of the Web.

3. The W3C must be sure the World Wide Web follows certain laws. The W3C must stay in contact with those in charge of laws and regulations. For example, they must be sure that Web users' personal information is protected.

4. The W3C wants to make sure people of all languages and cultural backgrounds are able to access the World Wide Web.

Prefixes

Knowing the meaning of the **prefix** of a new word can help you figure out the word's meaning. For example, the prefixes *con-* and *com-* often mean "with" or "together." Look at the word with the prefix *con-* in this sentence from "Weaving the World Together."

*The Internet provides the **connections** so the documents and files of the Web can be delivered where they are sent.*

The prefix *con-* and the context clues *delivered* and *sent* suggest that *connections* means "links between things." To link is to bring things *together*.

Read the following definitions of words that have *com-* or *con-* as a prefix. Think about how the prefix affects the meanings of the words.

com-municate = communicate = to share ideas and information **with** others

com-puter = computer = a machine that puts information **together**

com-plicated = complicated = mess up one thing **with** other things

con-sortium = consortium = people who work **together**

com-bine = combine = to join or mix **together**

Read the following sentences. On a separate sheet of paper, write the word from the list that completes each sentence.

complicated	combine	communicate
computer	consortium	

1. He designed the Web as a way to _____ documents.

2. In 1991, _____ users were first able to use the Web.

3. He is now in charge of the World Wide Web _____ .

4. He believes that the Web allows people to _____ and work together in ways no one imagined in years past.

5. If it broke up, communication between webs would be _____ and difficult.

Parody

A **parody** is a piece of work that copies another piece of work in a humorous way. The following verse is a parody of the song *The Ants Go Marching*. *The Ants Go Marching* is itself a parody of the Civil War song *When Johnny Comes Marching Home*. Practice reading it out loud to yourself with the correct rhythm. Then when you are ready, read it in a singsong way or sing it!

Read the lyrics and then sing them. Which do you like better? Which is easier? Which is more fun? Some people think that song melodies are easier to remember than lines of poetry. What do you think?

Marching Medley

We're surfing on the Internet. Hurrah! Hurrah!
We're surfing on the Internet. Hurrah! Hurrah!
We're surfing on the Internet.
There's so much help that we can get.
So we all go surfing—
Go online, have a good time,
Find lots of facts, then take a nap.

We chat with buddies on the Net. Hurrah! Hurrah!
We chat with buddies on the Net. Hurrah! Hurrah!
We chat with buddies on the Net
After our homework and chores are set.
Then we all go surfing—
Go online, have a good time,
Find lots of facts, then take a nap.

We all play games when we're online. Hurrah! Hurrah!
We all play games when we're online. Hurrah! Hurrah!
We all play games when we're online.
Grab a friend and have a good time.
And we all go surfing—
Go online, have a good time,
Find lots of facts, then take a nap.

Steps in a Process

How Television Works

You see a moving picture on television only because of how your brain works. Here is what happens.

1. A video camera takes a still picture (photograph) of what is happening. The camera takes 30 pictures, or frames, each second.

2. The camera turns each picture into rows of dots. Each dot, called a pixel, is a certain color and brightness.

3. Each row of pixels is sent across wires. The row is a series of electric signals.

4. The rows of pixels arrive at your TV set.

5. Your TV instantly puts the rows of pixels back in order.

6. When you look at the television screen, your eyes see rows of small colored dots.

7. Your brain changes these tiny dots into a meaningful picture.

8. The television shows the frames very quickly, one after the other.

9. Your brain changes the still pictures into a moving scene.

10. Your eyes see a moving picture.

Discussion Questions

Answer these questions with a partner or on a separate sheet of paper.

1. What is a pixel?

2. How is the picture sent from the TV studio to your television?
   a. as a series of frames
   b. as a series of still pictures
   c. as rows of dots
   d. as lines of color and brightness

3. What happens after the camera turns a still picture into rows of dots?
   a. Your TV turns the dots back into a picture.
   b. Your TV puts the rows of dots in order.
   c. Your eyes turn the rows of dots into a picture.
   d. The rows are sent across wires.

4. What would happen if your TV showed the frames very slowly?
   a. You would see rows of dots.
   b. You would see separate pictures.
   c. You would see electrical signals.
   d. You would see pixels.

5. What do you think would happen if the camera divided a picture into rows of large dots and sent those to your TV set?
   a. Your brain might not blend the large dots into a meaningful picture.
   b. Your eyes would see a bigger picture.
   c. Your eyes would see a still picture, not a moving one.
   d. The picture would seem to move more quickly.

6. Impressionism is a style of painting. It consists of dots of color that are painted separately and not mixed together. How is this like a televised picture?

7. Some computer printers work like television sets. How do these printers print a page of words?

8. Do you think television works too well? Would it be better if cameras and televisions could not transmit pictures to us so easily and clearly?

CONNECTING
to the Real World

EXPLORE MORE

Write a Nonfiction Story

Look at the time line in "A Real Television Hero." Select one of the inventions from the time line and research the inventor. Write a nonfiction story, similar to the one about Philo Farnsworth, about the inventor. Add photos and graphics.

Present a Sales Pitch

Research an inventor who was not included in this unit. Learn about his or her life in addition to the inventions. Write a monologue of the inventor trying to sell his invention to a manufacturer. Assume the role and present the monologue to the class. Be persuasive. Try to convince your classmates to purchase your invention. Tell them why it is a good invention, whom it will benefit, how it will be advertised, etc.

Write a Newspaper Article

One member of the class can take on the role of a reporter in the interview scenario. The reporter should write the answers to the interview in newspaper style. Add photos or illustrations.

Conduct an Interview

Choose a partner and carry out a biography-writing team project. Choose two inventors in history to interview. Both members of the team will develop a list of questions to ask during an interview. Then, each team member will assume the role of one of the inventors. Each team member will research the inventor he or she has become. Take turns interviewing the inventors using the questions you developed at the start.

Present a Photo Display

Choose an inventor or invention that was not included in this unit. Gather and copy photographs, illustrations, and other graphics about that choice. Present a photo display of the inventor and his or her invention to the class. Be sure to add captions and labels to your visuals.

Develop Your Own Invention!

Develop an invention of your own and present it to your classmates!

Related Books

Berners-Lee, Tim. *Weaving the Web: The Original Design and Ultimate Destiny of the World Wide Web.* HarperBusiness, 2000.

Cooney, Miriam P., ed. *Celebrating Women in Mathematics and Science.* National Council of Teachers of Mathematics, 1996.

Currie, Stephen. *Women Inventors.* Lucent Books, 2001.

Gaines, Ann. *Tim Berners-Lee and the Development of the World Wide Web.* Mitchell Lane Publishers, 2002.

Jeffrey, Laura S. *American Inventors of the 20th Century.* Enslow Publishers, Inc., 1996.

McClure, Judy. *Theoreticians and Builders: Mathematicians, Physical Scientists, Inventors.* Raintree Steck-Vaughn, 2000.

McPherson, Stephanie Sammartino. *TV's Forgotten Hero: The Story of Philo Farnsworth.* Carolrhoda Books, Inc., 1996.

Pasternak, Ceel. *Cool Careers for Girls in Computers.* Impact, 1999.

Roberts, Russell. *Philo T. Farnsworth: The Life of Television's Forgotten Inventor.* Mitchell Lane Publishers, 2004.

St. George, Judith. *So You Want to Be an Inventor?* Philomel Books, 2002.

Sullivan, Otha Richard. *African American Women Scientists and Inventors.* J. Wiley, 2002.

Thimmesh, Catherine. *Girls Think of Everything: Stories of Ingenious Inventions by Women.* Houghton Mifflin, 2000.

Wade, Mary Dodson. *Ada Byron Lovelace: The Lady and the Computer.* Dillon Press, 1994.

Interesting Web Sites

Philo Farnsworth

http://www.invent.org/hall_of_fame/56.html

http://inventors.about.com/library/inventors/blfarnsworth.htm

http://philotfarnsworth.com

http://www.time.com/time/time100/scientist/profile/farnsworth.html

Ada Byron

http://www.agnesscott.edu/lriddle/women/love.htm

http://www.well.com/user/adatoole/bio.htm

Tim Berners-Lee

http://www.ideafinder.com/history/inventors/berners-lee.htm

http://www.ibiblio.org/pioneers/lee.html

http://www.time.com/time/time100/scientist/profile/bernerslee.html

http://www.w3.org/People/Berners-Lee/

Web sites have been carefully researched for accuracy, content, and appropriateness. However, teachers and caregivers are reminded that Web sites are subject to change. Internet use should always be monitored.

Index

Index

Index

Index

Index

Index